# The
# **Road**
## to
# **Cultivate**
# **Yourself**

IRH PRESS

BOOKS
IRH PRESS
New York

ISBN 13: 978-1-958655-054
ISBN 10: 1-958655-05-8
Cover Image: 3D Vector/Shutterstock.com
aPhoenix photographer/Shutterstock.com
Sophia Williams/Shutterstock.com


Printed in Canada

First Edition

# The
# Road
## to
# Cultivate
# Yourself

FOLLOW YOUR SILENT VOICE WITHIN
TO GAIN TRUE WISDOM

# Ryuho Okawa

IRH PRESS

# *Contents*

Preface ........................ 13

CHAPTER ONE

# Follow Your Silent Voice

*Cultivate your inner mind and gain wisdom*

1 Thinking Differently in a Time of Stagnation ............... 16

2 The World Has Lost Its Sense of Direction

Is Japan more communist than China? ........................ 19

Democracy without God is no different from materialism ........ 22

3 Japan Will Have to Learn the "It's Enough" Mind

Japan is no longer a capitalist country ........................ 25

You won't see "rosy" economic growth anytime soon ............ 28

During a period of introspection, wipe your slate clean and
think about what is right ........................................ 30

Keep your desires from inflating and carefully choose things
of value ........................................................ 34

4 The Wisdom of Humanity You Should Learn in an Age of Collapsing Values

Refer back to the old times and think with your own head ... 37

Important things to learn in times of "staying indoors" .............. 41

a) Gaining both practical and general knowledge ................... 41

b) Studying classical works and foreign languages ................ 42

c) The Spirit World and the universe ................................... 43

In China, there is no freedom to learn various thoughts ............ 44

5 In Order to "Follow Your Silent Voice"

A right religion will cultivate a person's character and power of influence ................................................................. 48

There is no limit to developing your capacity as a person and your wisdom ................................................................. 51

6 Now Is the Time to Cultivate Your Inner Mind .............. 55

# CHAPTER TWO

# The Road to Cultivate Yourself
*Speaking on the essence of an intellectual life*

1   Preaching the Way of Life That You Should Know Now

What you should learn to live in society as a human being ... 60

Self-centered and conceited people cannot become a bodhisattva ................................................................ 61

2   It Is Difficult to Earn Credibility When You Are Young

Poems and novels that I could not publish during my youth ... 64

The difficulties of making a living from writing poems ................ 66

Why I decided to publish the poems and novels I wrote as a student ........................................................................... 68

*The Laws of the Sun* was rejected because of my age ................ 70

Shoichi Watanabe's frustrating experience publishing his first book ........................................................................... 73

You need to know the "common sense" of the industry ............ 75

In society, you will not be recognized for your talent alone ... 78

What to keep in mind if you are unsatisfied with the way you are treated ...................................................................... 79

People will not acknowledge you unless you are experienced, old, and accomplished ...................................................... 83

3   The Key to Becoming a Professional—Managing Time and Reading Books

The time I spent writing the novel *Chikyu Mangekyo* ............... 85

Are you efficiently reading books? ............................................. 87

4   A Cultivated Person Balances Intensive Reading with Extensive Reading

Intensive reading starts with careful study for entrance exams ... 90

Keep working on yourself until your talent blooms ................... 92

As a student, I had my thoughts printed on paper on two occasions ................................................................................ 94

Translating "Vox Populi, Vox Dei" from Japanese to English and vice versa helped me later on ........................................... 96

What I said shocked my professor at the university ................... 98

Balancing both intensive and extensive reading is the path to being a top-level expert ......................................................... 101

It takes willpower to do highly productive work ..................... 104

Making a habit of using small chunks of time for studying ... 106

5   Make Time to Be Alone and Take an Interest in Society

It is important for religious professionals to know about people's worries and sufferings ............................................. 110

Being attentive to society's suffering while being detached from society ........................................................................... 113

6   You Can Still Grow Regardless of Your Age

Relearning English from age 45 ............................................. 115

Precise and specialized English skills needed at the trading company ............................................................................... 119

7   The Importance of Making Decisions

Aim to become a topflight worker in your main work ............ 123

Doing well at practical work will help you to gain the trust
of others ........................................................................................................................ 124

The more spiritual you become, the more worldly effort you
will need to make ........................................................................................................ 125

You need to have common sense and make an effort to do
good work ...................................................................................................................... 128

8   How to Stay Active in Your Career

Take to heart that you will forget the things you have
learned ............................................................................................................................ 130

Do not become "tengu the conceited" but become
a bodhisattva ............................................................................................................... 132

Continue to work on your inner self to become a first-rate
person .............................................................................................................................. 135

CHAPTER THREE

# Spiritual Ability and the Right Way of Life

*The study of humans in the new era*

1  The Difficulty of Discerning Good and Evil in
   Spiritual Matters ........................................................................ 138

2  Focusing More on Your Inner-Self Rather Than on
   Appearance

   Many people are actually interested in spiritual matters ........ 140

   Happy Science has been focusing on its content since
   the beginning ........................................................................ 141

   Why I dismissed the idea of a uniform ................................. 144

3  Fighting Off Spiritual Hindrance and Ensuring
   Quality Control

   I seemed like a bookworm but had a surprising skill in my
   student days ........................................................................ 146

   Some will spiritually awaken by studying my books and
   lectures ........................................................................ 148

   The feeling of a "spiritual current" running through you ........ 150

   An open spiritual channel does not mean almighty power ...... 152

4   Spiritual Ability Must Come with Greater Insight and
    Learning

A psychologist cannot medically examine someone more
highly regarded than them ................................................................ 156

Answering questions on topics from management to
black holes ........................................................................................ 158

The required studies to offer opinions to various leaders ......... 160

5   A Religious Professional Must Be a Person of Great
    Culture and Knowledge

Stating your thoughts while keeping in mind the opposite
opinion .............................................................................................. 163

What was lacking in the leaders of new Japanese religions? ... 165

Intelligence alone does not make you a good religious leader ... 168

6   Be Humble and Take One Firm Step at a Time

Do not become tengu for having spiritual abilities ..................... 170

The consequences of using your intelligence for selfish
reasons .............................................................................................. 172

Religion is a comprehensive study of humans ............................ 174


Afterword ................ 177

About the Author ......................................................... 181

What Is El Cantare? ..................................................... 182

Books by Ryuho Okawa .............................................. 184

Happy Science's English Sutra .................................... 192

Music by Ryuho Okawa .............................................. 193

About Happy Science .................................................. 194

Happy Science University ............................................ 196

Contact Information ..................................................... 198

About IRH Press USA ................................................. 200

# *Preface*

With this book, the total number of my publications is 3,000. The first book published was *Spiritual Messages from Saint Nichiren* at the end of July 1985, so it has taken about 37 years to come this far.

The life I have been living is very much represented by the title of this book—*The Road to Cultivate Yourself.* Although I, myself, will not judge the level of the content of these 3,000 books, they are the most published works in the world by a single author—in other words, they can be called the modern Tripitaka, the tremendous volume of Buddhist scriptures.

What is spoken in this book is what I believe and think; it reveals my true heart. I believe that I, myself, would also be causing trouble to society if I were to move people and give influence without having to train myself.

Our world is full of apocalyptic events—the worldwide coronavirus pandemic, the Russia-Ukraine war, the crisis of yet another world war, and the imminent great depression. The only way to get through them is to polish your wisdom. I hope this book serves as a painful yet vital lesson for the better.

*Ryuho Okawa*
*Master & CEO of Happy Science Group*
*April 29, 2022*

---

\* As of April 2023, the total number of the author's publications has surpassed 3,100.

# CHAPTER ONE

# Follow Your Silent Voice

## —Cultivate your inner mind and gain wisdom

Originally recorded in Japanese on September 9, 2021, at the Special Lecture Hall of Happy Science in Japan and later translated into English.

# 1

# Thinking Differently
# in a Time of Stagnation

Currently, I feel that the great majority of people are feeling quite lost about how they should live regarding their occupations, daily life, and relationships. People are also feeling quite lost about how they should perceive or think about things. As we are in such times, let's return to the main road of religion and reorganize our way of thinking.

As you can see from current affairs, the coronavirus pandemic has continued for almost two years now (as of this lecture). Although some say things are getting back to normal, we should not let our guard down anytime soon.

Nevertheless, I don't want to predict a negative future too much; doing so will not benefit us but only keep us from fully carrying out our activities. On the other hand, this is not the time to predict a bright future merely based on positive thinking. The current situation does not allow me to say, "As things are at their worst now, they will only improve from now on."

So I suggest we think a little differently.

For example, Japan has been, in a way, stagnant for 20-30 years now, but here is some food for thought: Japan experienced almost 300 years of stagnation in the Edo period (1603-1867). The economy did occasionally improve, but many catastrophic events occurred, such as famines, plagues, earthquakes, tsunamis, and volcanic eruptions. Also, the social system itself did not encourage growth; back then, Japan's basic policies were to preserve the status quo.

This system collapsed during *bakumatsu*, the final years of the Edo period. Some traders became wealthy by smuggling or trading with foreign countries and began to hold a greater share of power. Until then, agriculture was the main industry of the Japanese economy, and rice was used as currency. But when the merchants became more powerful, they grew wealthier because they did not have to pay high taxes. In that way, the times changed, and it is how the social system collapsed.

That was Japan's nearly 300-year period of stagnation. The current period of stagnation is only about one-tenth as long as the period back then. Politicians may say various things such as, "We will get out of deflation" or "We will enter a period of rapid growth again," but that may not happen. In any case, you should know that, as history shows, humans experience periods of stagnation from time to time.

What is more, worldly common sense and worldly ways of thinking do not last for long. One example of this is the population of Japan. The birthrate has halved since my generation. Another example is that prior to the 2020 Tokyo Olympics, some people were saying that children would not be affected by the coronavirus. So they were suggesting that children should be allowed inside the stadium to watch the games while adults should not. But soon after, the virus started to spread even among the youth, so nurseries, preschools, elementary schools, etc., were considering closing their facilities temporarily.

# 2

## The World Has Lost
## Its Sense of Direction

### Is Japan more communist than China?

In the final years of the 20th century, the United States was believed to continue to lead the world as the greatest superpower for another 100 or 200 years. However, just 20 years into the 21st century, it is showing clear signs of decline. That is how I have analyzed the current situation.

The "challengers" of the United States are China—which claims to be a communist country—and the Muslim world. This is also very clear. From now on, there will be conflicts and competition between differing values.

Let us look at China, who is one of the challengers. It also has problems. China is a communist country based on materialist and atheist thinking, but here is something I thought about the other day. When I have some spare time, I sometimes watch a television program on Chinese conversation. The program showed that there are many ethnic minorities in China and that in the southern part of Sichuan Province is a village of an ethnic minority called the Yi. I was surprised at how the NHK (Japan Broadcasting Corporation) was able to broadcast such a program. I guess the Beijing government already had too much on its plate to censor the program. In this village, each family lived on an average annual income of ¥100,000 ($700). They are so poor that they cannot afford to get an education. The TV program was telling a story, in an emotionally touching style, about how a teacher came to this village to teach but left after two years, only to then return. "Isn't China the second largest economic power in the world?" "Isn't its GDP double that of Japan?" Such thoughts crossed my mind.

Sichuan Province, which is close to the main home of pandas, is the navel of China. Nevertheless, the Yi, who live there, are poor, maybe because they are a minority. Regardless, I thought, "Are there any households in Japan that could live on an income of ¥100,000 per year?" Of course, if you are homeless, you would have to live like that. The point is those people are living in a barter economy or a "beggars' economy." They are not living in a monetized economy. In Japan, you can usually receive more than ¥100,000 per year even if you are not working. You can apply for welfare and receive a little more than that. So you probably will not be as poor as those Chinese minorities when living in Japan. That is why I thought, "Wait, isn't communism about making everyone equal?"

The rich in China probably own trillions, hundreds of billions, or tens of billions of yen; even a mayor can accumulate tens of billions of yen. But then there is a village where its entire population lives on an annual income of ¥100,000 per household. A similar time to this in Japan would be around 1945, when the country was devastated after World War II, or a little before the war.

There is a severe wealth gap in China. Therefore, this contradiction of China will cause the country to fall apart, no matter what it may say. That is because what China does goes completely against the communist ideology.

In fact, Japan is more of a "communist" country than China, so some people in Japan are condemned as "privileged people." Those who can get COVID vaccine shots when others cannot, or those who can be admitted into the hospital when everyone else cannot, are criticized as "privileged people."

On another note, some people are snooping around the Japanese royal family and making comments such as, "It's outrageous for Princess Mako to receive ¥140 million to leave the royal family," and "She said she will decline the money, but apparently, she can still receive ¥100 million for different reasons."

These instances show that Japan is just like a communist country. It is astonishing. A communist country is like the "crabs in a bucket," where the crabs at the bottom of the bucket drag down other crabs that try to escape. So in reality,

Japan is more like a communist country, whereas the "main" communist country (China) is actually not communist. Over there, some dictators, authorities, and entourages are enjoying their privileges.

By the way, in the Korean Peninsula, namely South Korea, whenever a new president is inaugurated, the former president either is executed, commits suicide, is massacred along with the entire family, or has their assets stripped away. It is as if they are still living in the Sengoku period (the civil war period in Japan, from the latter half of the 15th century to the latter half of the 16th century). Similar things occur in Southeast Asia, too.

## Democracy without God is no different from materialism

In August (2021), U.S. troops withdrew from Afghanistan, and within about two weeks, the Taliban took control. I have seen in the newspapers that the Taliban will establish the Ministry for the Propagation of Virtue and the Prevention of Vice. Frankly, it was so ironic that my face froze. I guess a religion should not ridicule something like this.

On one level, it is truly brilliant and wonderful to be able to propagate virtue and prevent vice at the ministry level. It would be amazing if something like this was established in Japan, too. However, the question is, what will the Taliban do in the name of "propagating virtue and preventing vice"? We will have to wait and see.

Although I do not want to become just an "observer," I can neither support nor oppose Islam until I see what they do over a longer period of time. What do they consider *good*, and what do they consider *evil*? Over the next year or so, their true thoughts will become visible and transparent. "What is their true criterion for what is good and what is evil?" "What would truly happen if they acted in accordance with their fundamental teachings?" I will be watching closely to see whether their thoughts are in accordance with God's or Allah's teachings. This is where their values clash with those of Western society.

Looking at Western countries, Mr. Biden does not have much to say other than to talk about human rights. However, the idea of human rights itself has been considerably changing and is not fixed, so we still cannot tell how it will turn out.

There are many issues in the new idea of "human rights" that I am especially concerned about. So I am not sure whether such "human rights" should be protected. The idea of "propagating virtue and preventing vice" is lacking in the West, as is an understanding of what is right and wrong in God's eyes. So these concepts are not part of the West's idea of "human rights," and they just advocate protecting people's rights, such as the right to survive and the right to live.

What I mean is that if you disregard good and evil from the metaphysical, theoretical, or philosophical point of view and only advocate for this diminished idea of "human rights," then "human rights" will become similar to materialism. People will start caring more about things such as food, housing, and the convenience of living and will ultimately seek materialistic values only.

It has become extremely difficult to tell which direction the world will eventually head in. In any case, much of democracy has become "democracy without God," and it has become difficult to differentiate democracy from materialism.

From here, people might start rioting, turn society into a "safari park," and start living instinctively like animals.

# 3

## Japan Will Have to Learn the "It's Enough" Mind

### Japan is no longer a capitalist country

The world is in such difficult times. Regarding Japan, the country is not growing in the economic sense. In terms of people's income, their wages are not increasing despite Japan being one of the developed countries. Thus, it seems that Japan has lost all hope as well.

On the other hand, there is a trend to waive tuition in elementary schools, junior high schools, high schools, and universities. This may cause the economy to shrink. Perhaps Japan is aiming to become a society that does not need money.

Nowadays, I hear some people say that, in a way, the value of money in Japan has gone back to how it was in the Stone Age. Even if you have money saved in your bank account, it does not accrue interest, and you are left with the amount you deposited. That is the reality of today.

In a purely capitalist world, people with money will naturally do things such as start a business and make a profit or will become rich by buying land or constructing a building or a factory. But currently, in Japan, even if people have money, it makes no difference. Banks are unable to find people who will take out a loan. I guess people are not thinking of taking out loans because they have no way to use the money. That is the current reality. People seem to be just fine with teleworking from home and having food delivered to them through something like Uber Eats, so I am worried about how things will turn out.

Therefore, our idea of money is reverting back to how it was during the Stone Age, when money was made out of stones. I think this shows how Japan is slowly becoming a non-capitalist country.

If this is the case, what does it mean? Like the example of the Tokugawa period (Edo period) I gave earlier, we may have to endure a period of time where you must know contentment—in other words, times when the only way to get by will be to practice the "It's Enough" mind. This is possible. The birth rate in Japan is declining, and the elderly population is increasing. About one-third of the Japanese population is over 65 years of age, and people's life expectancy is increasing.

Life expectancy and healthy life expectancy are different. It seems that, on average, more people fall ill at around 75 years of age and become hospitalized 5–10 years after that. Therefore, the government will need to spend its tax money mostly on hospitalization, medicine, treatment, and hospital beds. Then, tax money will only be spent, with no increase in government revenue. I am not sure whether you can call this a "consumer economy."

But the fact is that COVID is spreading, and healthcare workers are fleeing from workplaces one after another. Their work is "dirty, demanding, and dangerous." It is not very pleasant. It must be hard seeing corpses all the time, and they may have had enough of seeing sick people all the time.

Moreover, patients with diseases other than COVID are not going to the doctor or the hospital as much as usual. Patients with serious illnesses such as cancer, heart disease, lung disease, or brain disease avoid going to the doctor or hospital because they think they will catch COVID if they do. I thought doctors and hospitals were making a little profit because of COVID, but that does not seem to be the case.

Even though the Japanese government's 2022–2023 fiscal budget is over ¥100 trillion ($780 billion), the government is saying that ¥33 trillion ($260 billion) of it will be spent on medical expenses, including COVID-related matters. In addition, it has to pay maturity redemption for government bonds and the accrued interest—about ¥30 trillion in total. So the government needs to pay around ¥63 trillion for government bonds, or the government's debt, plus the medical budget. I wonder whether this country will be able to survive.

## You won't see "rosy" economic growth anytime soon

Looking at the current state of Japan as a whole, this is what I must say now: politicians and others may say various things, but a "rosy" revival of economic growth is not likely to happen anytime soon.

After World War II, Japan's domestic economy was devastated, but the country was able to develop in the post-war period because it put more energy into foreign trade. Unfortunately, it has become difficult to trade between countries because people are unable to travel freely between them. This year, trading companies have been making considerable profits mainly on natural resources, which has meant that these resources have experienced a jump in their prices. However, you should know that these are not stable earnings. I am unsure as to what will happen from now on, but the least I can say is, it is very unlikely for the economy to expand through trading or tourism in an age where it is not easy to move between countries.

We must read the trends of this age. When thinking about various things, one thing that comes to mind is that because of COVID, we cannot go outdoors or cannot go to work, and despite having to stay home, the infection rate at home has risen. It also rose at schools.

In addition, we have been seeing a lot of rain this year in Japan, so the price of vegetables is soaring. There has been heavy rainfall owing to the linear precipitation zone, which has then brought floods. Floods were also seen in Germany and China, and there were scenes in New York on TV that I had never seen before: the news said this kind of flooding is expected to occur once in a 200–500-year period, but this is as far as the entire history of the United States goes. It just means that this kind of downpour has never been seen before in the United States. Of course, that is true. There was no subway back then, so it was impossible to have an underground flood. But nowadays, there are subways, and the rainwater is overflowing and gushing out.

If Manhattan gets flooded, as the city itself is at sea level, everything will be underwater. I am uncertain whether the upper floors of buildings will be safe, but if power generators and other devices stop working, people will not be able to do anything. Buildings usually have self-powered generators, which are usually located in the basement. The control room for generators and boilers is also typically found in the basement, so once it is flooded, even a skyscraper will stop working, and the people inside will be left stranded.

So the situation now is quite serious.

## During a period of introspection, wipe your slate clean and think about what is right

Considering the above, I feel humanity is being told to "start over" again. Epidemics, as well as floods, wildfires, earthquakes, tsunamis, and possibly volcanic eruptions, will increasingly occur. I feel we are being told to start over.

What does this mean? I think that a period of introspection will come once again, but that is not necessarily a bad thing.

There may be times when people are able to easily earn money in this world or when they become very extroverted and go out to all kinds of places—sightseeing and traveling. There may be times when someone takes out a loan to buy an apartment building, and its value doubles after a year. In such times, people can lose themselves in pursuing profit from these things. Nowadays, people are also making a lot of money just by buying or selling things online. If these things continue for too long, people will lose sight of the solid work ethic that they should have as human beings. Therefore, stagnation and poverty can have some degree of a tightening effect on people.

The basic pattern is that after a period like this, there will be a kind of breakthrough. Those who can pave their way to the next age will appear, and the times will change. Therefore, for a while, you should be thinking about how to get through tough times.

In particular, you must deeply think about controlling your desires. People living in Western democratic societies are being controlled by their desires. It seems that they do not think about whether their desires are good or evil and are apt to establish policies that affirm those desires. Although there are debates going on over these policies, we do not see good results in any of them.

Therefore, as I said earlier, it is as if we are given a *koan* (a contemplative question in Zen Buddhism): "Wipe the slate clean and think again. What do you think is right? What do you think you should do?"

Some Japanese critics are called "intellectual giants" in newspapers and magazines, but in my eyes, they do not appear that way at all. What they are doing is processing information. Information is overflowing, so processing it all has become tedious. That is why those who can process information in their head without using a device appear to be intellectual giants.

But just how much value is there to the information these people talk about? We must examine it with particular care. Everyone knows that most of the day-to-day information we receive is unnecessary. The value of information in morning newspapers is lost by evening. The information becomes useless the next day, and it becomes garbage by the weekend. Moreover, the same information is dispatched to different forms of media. Everyone kills time by looking at the same information in newspapers, on TV, and on their phones—again and again. We will soon enter an age when bad content will be dismissed and will fade out.

Unnecessary and meaningless economic activities will also be eliminated, which is not a bad thing. For example, John Lennon's spirit mentioned something like the following: "Regarding music, it is OK for good artists to gather big audiences. But there are many questionable artists who gather large crowds at venues like stadiums and make money. If I may say so, I'd be grateful if they fail." (See Chapter Two in *Shakyamuni Buddha's Future Prediction*.)

Everything seems good when the economy is up, money is circulating well, and society is prospering. However, in those times, people will easily judge something as good. It means people can make a profit from doing pretty much anything. They will spend time and money like water

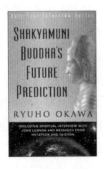

*Shakyamuni Buddha's Future Prediction*
(Tokyo: HS Press, 2020)

just to satisfy themselves. But we are now facing serious repercussions regarding these easy judgments and wasteful ways of life.

In the 1990s, Japan crushed the economic bubble, and the mass media said the "economic bubble burst." Those in the mass media probably thought that the burst economy would end after two or three years. The thought of it continuing for over 30 years did not even cross their mind. I presume they did not anticipate that it also meant that the mass media would collapse.

Some printed newspapers have halved their circulation since their peak, and some magazines have gone bankrupt. To be blunt, I think that many TV programs are needless as well. I feel bad saying this, but we have reached the point where no one would care even if the news aired for only an hour a day—perhaps like in North Korea. People do not know what to spend their time on.

So we will have to consider the question, "If we were to go back in time a little and rethink how we should live, what should we do?" But going back in time does not mean we will return to the early 20th-century life depicted in *Oshin* (a Japanese TV drama series). Because the basic infrastructure and technologies are highly developed, things like buildings and facilities will not utterly vanish. This is a basic point that I would like you to keep in mind.

## Keep your desires from inflating
## and carefully choose things of value

If you focus too much on just worldly progress and prosperity, your thinking will grow closer to materialism. Think about it. Making millions or tens of millions of yen by playing with numbers does seem like a more exciting way of living than reading books or attending seminars at religious institutions. More people will probably be drawn to this exciting way of life.

However, you should know that this way of life does not add anything to your intellect. Suppose you made millions of yen—let's say five million yen—a day through day trading. In doing so, did you make something worth the five million yen profit you made or something productive for humanity, society, or the world? No, you did not. You did not produce anything. It is just like winning in a game of numbers.

There are companies where people make profits by transferring money, playing with numbers, or selling and buying stocks as if playing a video game. In other words, a large percentage of people are making money through "virtual businesses." They may seem to be making a profit now, but an economy where real businesses decline but virtual businesses grow is absolutely wrong. Therefore, I am sure that everyone will eventually leave virtual businesses.

We should refer back to the olden days and be strict with ourselves. We need to consider, "Is this something worth doing? By doing so, does it contribute to the progress of humanity or add something positive to make society affluent in the truest sense?"

Another point of concern is the issue of productivity in Japanese politics. Just highlighting the problems will not solve anything. However, there are many politicians now, and some repeatedly talk about how the economy will recover. If these politicians become prime ministers, they will definitely be called liars and driven out.

Here is what I want to say:

People's desires unknowingly grow as material things fill the world and people are taken over by them. As your desires grow, it becomes extremely difficult to purify your mind, make your mind transparent, or contemplate a world that is not of this earthly world.

There is a Japanese word, *ganbutsu-soshi*, which means that you will forget your aspiration if you become engrossed in materials. In this way, adults are also like children; children try hard to get the toys they want, but as they keep getting them, they forget what they were originally aspiring to do.

That is what happens in society when we have too many material things and are taken over by them. So we must carefully choose which things are valuable and utilize, produce, buy, or sell them. That is what will be important in the coming age.

# 4

## The Wisdom of Humanity You Should Learn in an Age of Collapsing Values

### Refer back to the old times and think with your own head

As for me, I have experienced the Showa period (1926-1988). Back then, I was often told, "You are a person of the Taisho period (1912-1926), the cultural age of the Taisho period," or "You are a man from 50 years ago." Therefore, as we are currently in the Reiwa period, it might be good for you to refer back to how people lived during the Showa period. Then, you must ask: What are this world's notions of common sense and morals? What should people aim for in life?

For example, how were things back when I was in elementary school? The most popular career for girls was a stewardess, now known as a cabin attendant. I remember that becoming a stewardess was a popular career. I cannot recall what the most popular career was for boys, but I think there were many. When I was in elementary school, not many boys dreamed of becoming professional athletes. Maybe it became popular a little later on.

Then, a period of rapid growth led to people investing more money into education, thinking that they could give their children a head start by branding them with their school's name. That is how some schools became known as prestigious schools. This was then followed by a period of spending money on cram schools, with rich mothers in Mercedes picking up their children or bringing a bento for them at cram schools. That was perceived as having high status. I believe this was when my children were in elementary school. But such a trend is also in decline now.

Oftentimes, I compare how things are now with how they were a generation ago. What is the difference between now and then? One might be that for some time, we were brainwashed into believing that the future will be secure for those who have acquired the status of being smart or of graduating from a prestigious school. But this status itself was something created by humans.

This "entry ticket" idea is likely to fail you in an age where companies decline and go bankrupt one after another. This is also an age where companies might not survive just by doing the same work, even if they have been doing well for 100 years.

What is necessary is to return to the olden times and rethink how people used to live (like the Japanese people in the Showa period). Wise are those who have the ability to think with their own heads when they encounter something for the first time.

Cram schools teach students how to analyze exam questions as patterns; they teach them techniques to solve questions according to patterns. People thought that spending money to study these would favorably work in passing entrance exams. That meant you could get qualifications or a good educational background, which would secure the pathway to climb up the career ladder. However, this kind of thinking is already coming to an end.

Take, for example, the University of Tokyo. Studying at the Faculty of Law and becoming a government official was considered the most prestigious career. But now, such careers mean nothing to students, so fewer of them are seeking that path. Nowadays, they have shifted toward thinking that the elites are those who study at the Faculty of Economics and then go on to earn money by selling or buying nonsensical things at foreign companies.

However, most of these elites who sell and buy intangible things by playing with numbers on a computer screen are not suited for that kind of career in the first place, so they will eventually "die out." They will only do well in the beginning. They may make lots of profit at the start, but that is it. Most of them are never heard of again. They are not suited for this type of work.

In fact, the professors who taught those people are not suited for that kind of work themselves. Most of them are busy interpreting the classics or focusing on trivial matters; they cannot give their opinion on current affairs. If these are the people who taught you, you most likely will not be able to manage such a job.

From now on, it will be very difficult to find a so-called elite course. Things will be tough in whichever field you may choose. What was considered powerful or had authority will no longer be effective, and you will not be able to tell what is advantageous. Even if you think that a certain field of work is a trend and jump into it, it might go downhill. I think we are heading into such an age.

Therefore, we must go back to the fundamental truths of human existence and think about why we were born, why we live on earth, and what work awaits us after we leave this earthly world. With those things considered, we must understand the conditions we live in and think about how to live our lives. We are living in an age where what is considered valuable in this world will soon collapse.

## Important things to learn
## in times of "staying indoors"

### a) Gaining both practical and general knowledge

I have spoken about the importance of thinking and dealing with things using your own head.

Until now, many businesses sold the idea that as long as you learn the winning patterns, you will easily get into an elite course and progress up the career ladder, or you will secure an "express ticket" for promotions. But I think almost all of these kinds of thinking will become useless.

I dare say that those who can "punt in the stream"—or who can step back, look across all times and places through their own eyes, and figure out what must be done—will be the only ones to come out victorious in the coming age.

If so, what important things should you learn during this time? Of course, the times are changing even as we live now, so you should have a sufficient understanding of current affairs. It would not be a smart move to completely ignore what is going on now. Becoming useless in today's society will lead to problems. You should, more or less, know about what is happening in the present. You must also make use of things that can be used now, such as practical and general knowledge.

## b) Studying classical works and foreign languages

Another thing to learn during this time is the human wisdom contained in ancient ages that has stood the test of time. So if you are spending more and more time at home, now is the time to reread classical works. What are the values that have survived through the ages? You need to find them in classical works.

Also, to gain insights, you will absolutely need to learn about foreign cultures. You need to be able to see Japan's current state or how people live in Japan from the perspective of other cultures.

Language is one of the tools to gain this perspective. You can simply study a foreign language to communicate with others, but you should not just stop there. Through that language, you should dig deeper and learn the culture and history of the countries that use it. This is important because there are connections between a country's language and its culture.

While you acquire the perspective of another country, you will also need to learn about Japan. You should know what kinds of things occurred in Japanese history, re-examine current Japan from the newly gained perspective of "virtue and vice" that I mentioned earlier, and observe how Japan appears to be. If you have a perspective like this, you will be able to see things from a viewpoint far beyond that of the current age.

## c) The Spirit World and the universe

Yet another topic to learn about is the other world, which is what religion teaches. This is somewhat difficult to do, as there are only a few people left who can teach about it. Nonetheless, at Happy Science, we have been teaching about the updated, modern-day affairs of the Spirit World. Studying about the other world means you are learning in advance before you go there. This is also essential in thinking about the way you should live now.

Happy Science is also releasing information about extraterrestrial beings. However, I understand this is quite a controversial topic. When it comes to things like aliens and UFOs, various information is going around in society, but very little of it is trustworthy. Perhaps it is like the stories in the world of *yokai* (monsters and goblins). Most people who are interested in UFOs and aliens and provide information about them are not trusted in terms of their work or their character.

It is fine for people who can properly think, process things, and act to be interested in and be educated about UFOs and aliens to a certain extent. But if people who have no skills in matters related to this earthly world are interested in extraterrestrial matters only, they will end up being useless in society.

If people like these were to be useful, it would be in producing manga, anime, or some types of novels. Interest in UFOs, aliens, and the universe may help to enhance their creativity in fiction. But if taken in the wrong way, the Spirit World and the universe could be seen as the genre of last resort for these "social outcasts." So we must be very careful about these matters.

## In China, there is no freedom to learn various thoughts

I have talked about studying a foreign language. However, what is very convenient in Japan is that you can read about pretty much anything in Japanese. Most writings are translated into Japanese, and more people in Japan can now read English to some degree.

In China, Xi Jinping is currently working very hard in the field of education to spread the Beijing dialect, which uses simplified Chinese characters, all across China. Simplified Chinese is a phonetic language rather than an ideographic one—in other words, it is about the sound. But in terms of sound or pronunciation, Chinese characters cannot beat the alphabet. Simplified Chinese can never beat the conciseness of the alphabet.

In fact, compared with traditional Chinese characters, simplified Chinese characters have lost the unique depth where various characters are used based on subtle differences in meaning. That is why I think that the Chinese people nowadays are less intelligent. Chinese people may not have been as simple-minded long ago, but to speak bluntly, that is how they are now.

One of the things I am grateful for is that I was born a Japanese person. Thanks to that, I can read ancient Chinese classics (because the Japanese and Chinese scripts share common characters). Although Chinese people nowadays cannot read these classics, a Japanese person like me can read them.

Most Chinese people can only read simplified Chinese, so they cannot read their own classical literature. That is why it is easy to brainwash them through education. If current Chinese politicians want to lead their people in a certain direction, they just need to write their ideas using simplified Chinese and make people think only about the sound. And as long as people can communicate daily using simplified Chinese, this will be enough. This type of education has resulted in Chinese people no longer being able to read Chinese classics. So they cannot freely study different thoughts of the past.

Instead, if you are Japanese, you can read Chinese classics without any footnotes or commentary or by changing the order of characters and adding words to make it understandable. You can also read the translated version, whether it is in traditional Japanese or modern Japanese.

So there are four ways that Japanese people can read Chinese classics.

When I went to Singapore and Malaysia in Southeast Asia, I read a Chinese newspaper written in traditional Chinese, which uses a more complicated set of kanji characters originating from hieroglyphs. I skimmed through it and could understand about 70 percent of its content.

This rarely happens to me with other non-English newspapers, so I thought about how amazing it is to be able to understand a foreign language just by looking at the characters. The characters present you with a large amount of information, so you can understand what the articles are about at a glance.

This kind of education is what is lacking among the current Chinese people, which is why they can be brainwashed into believing whatever the leaders want them to. There are fewer and fewer intelligent people.

Further, in Shanghai, exams are currently being abolished from English education. English will soon become the "language of the enemy," and fewer Chinese students will study abroad. If that is the case, China will presumably become an entirely brainwashed nation.

The Chinese population is also slightly decreasing. In fact, the Indian population is larger. India has around 1.4 billion people, whereas China seems to have less than 1.4 billion. In addition, although the elderly make up a large percentage of the population in China, India still has a large population of young people. Last but not least, Indian people can speak English and another language, possibly Hindi or something else. So I believe India has a higher potential for development.

That being said, it is indeed important to learn the language of the country with the highest cultural level at the time. You can get a job that is related to studying "dead" languages, such as Latin or Ancient Greek, which can be good training for the brain. You can also make a living by becoming a teacher or researcher of those languages, but that is about it. Otherwise, it may be difficult for you to make a living using "dead" languages.

I believe that Japan can extend its influence even more if its people can have the right mindset. Japanese people have the means to understand and integrate the areas of Western culture, Chinese culture, and Islamic culture that I previously mentioned. That is why, with the right mindset, Japanese culture could become the new mainstream culture.

If possible, I would like people in Southeast Asia and Africa to study Japanese properly, and the same goes for India and Brazil. If more and more people can speak Japanese, we will draw closer to our goal. I believe so.

# 5

# In Order to
# "Follow Your Silent Voice"

## A right religion will cultivate
## a person's character and power of influence

I gave this chapter the title, "Follow Your Silent Voice," which is very close to *zen* (禅). In the same way that I raised the topic of "intellectual giants" earlier, the question I am now asking is, "What is true intellect?"

How should you consider those who cannot look within their minds or do not know what their minds are? What about those who cannot delve into their minds and connect to the high spirits in the Real World, to their guardian or guiding spirits, or to the road leading to God?

As mentioned before, people nowadays call out, "The privileged people are...." They are talking about worldly privileges, such as economic privileges. But that is not the point. I have been teaching that by connecting to the Real World, you can attain various ways of thinking, philosophies, and things that will have a positive effect on yourself and your future. But if you stay completely detached from the Real World and only think about how to gain advantages and increase your profits in this world, you will lose out in the world that awaits you after death.

The world of hell is certainly expanding now. Imagine if you lived thinking, "I did well in this world. I lived a life that people would dream of living," but fell to hell after you died. This is just so foolish. If you knew this would happen, you would have lived your life differently. You would have lived a completely different life from the very start. Unfortunately, people are not able to do this.

For example, it is said that in Japan, those who grew up watching Japanese folklore on evening TV programs have a relatively high interest in the other world and faith. Materialists increased in number after folklore stopped being aired on TV. Most people who grew up without encountering faith or mystical matters such as the Real World or the Spirit World during their educational years from childhood to adulthood completely disregard these things after they become adults. It is sad, but no matter how much we convey the Truth to them, oftentimes, it ends up as a wasted effort. This is very disappointing.

What would be the worst is for people to consider laws made by the Diet as the highest authority and simply obey them. This is no different from what is happening with the Chinese Communist Party. Because they think there is no God, the law is everything to them. If laws are created to favor patriots, political freedom will ultimately be lost. They do not make laws to deprive people of political freedom but make laws that favor patriots. This leads to the loss of political freedom. That is how things will turn out.

What can you ultimately rely on? What things can you rely on even when society changes? The answer is the values that have been established in the Real World. The values that are not yet fixed in the Real World cannot be relied on.

In general, religions are strongly disliked because some new, large religions are misguided. Among the religions that officially claim to have millions of believers are some religions that are clearly misguided. People may look at someone from a misguided religion and instinctively or spiritually feel, "Something seems wrong. Ever since he joined *that* religious group, he has gone crazy." Unfortunately, some people reject religion precisely because there are religious groups whose members often become odd after joining them.

In essence, if people can separate wrong from right and move closer to what is right, they should become better people, refine their character, have a higher reputation among others, and be a good influence on others. You must carefully look at the "fruits" that religions bear. Something is wrong with religions whose believers lie and deceive others all the time.

Recently, just as I expected, I have come to understand more than ever that politicians must be able to lie if they want to survive in Japanese politics. It is becoming the norm for politicians to be able to lie. They knowingly exchange lies with each other, and those who can lie better survive in the political world. That is how it seems to be. Those who are caught and have their lies exposed have to resign. That is why they must become cunning and make sure they do not make inappropriate remarks. Therefore, Japanese politics is not based on true speech. If politicians spoke the truth, the Diet would operate more smoothly. In a way, politicians are acknowledged for their skills at lying through manipulating words, but this is poor politics. It must be reformed soon.

## There is no limit to developing your capacity as a person and your wisdom

Overall, there are many things you can do, but it is especially important to cultivate yourself with different kinds of knowledge and, to exercise your brain, study practical subjects.

Nonetheless, this is what I want to say in general. It is important to ensure more people can go back to the starting point and think from a clean slate whether something is worth doing—and if doing so adds to their true knowledge—and whether their success in this is a plus to this world and the other world.

These things must be done as a religious activity, of course, and if education and the mass media have the wrong answers to those questions, they must be corrected.

In particular, in modern-day education, students who do not go to religiously affiliated schools all graduate without knowing even the slightest element of the Truth. Those students often end up as the elites of this world, which is very dangerous.

Some scholars who were wrong in terms of the Truth and improper as human beings are sent to hell. At best, most of the other scholars who were not evil—in other words, those who were good—return to the lower level of the sixth dimension in the Spirit World. Some of them return to the fifth dimension, but most of them go to the lower level of the sixth dimension. They are the ones who make the exam questions for things such as entrance exams, mock exams, and certification exams. So these exams cannot tell whether the exam takers have a higher level of awareness than those scholars.

That is why those scholars cannot teach about the acts of bodhisattvas, tathagatas, or the Will of God and Buddha at all, which are things that Happy Science teaches. What is being taught in education is far below that level. The only way is for religions to teach about these things, so we must work hard. Even philosophy is far behind now and is very far from the Truth. There were righteous philosophies in ancient times, but in this age, there are very few true ones.

Therefore, we must strongly point out, push, and spread what is truly valuable.

People have been saying that thanks to quarantines, they are reading more books. Some are even saying that adults are reading picture books. But you will find many "junk" books as well. Junk will remain junk, no matter how much of it you read. So you need to be able to discern junk from things of good quality.

I, myself, want to be the "royal road" of good quality. By reading both Happy Science books and other books, you will be able to check the quality of the other books and either accept or reject them.

Do not waste your time on useless things. Rather than reading a junk book, you might as well be lost in thought or go for a walk. I earnestly recommend you quit absorbing wrong ideas or spending most of your day doing meaningless things.

There is a lot to teach about the mind, but educational institutions nowadays do not teach you how to correct your mind. So I would like you to know more about how to do this.

Your body may grow, but your height and weight will stop increasing at a certain point; there is a limit. But as for the realm of the mind, there is a lot of room for expansion.

There is still plenty of room for your capacity, or caliber, and your wisdom to grow. In fact, this is essential in every age.

So I would like you to return to the main road of religion. In this current age, where we will see the bubble burst economy continue, please keep speaking up, again and again, about what is true and what is important. I will also do so.

# 6

# Now Is the Time to Cultivate Your Inner Mind

In this age, we will continue to experience many tough events for a while, but you should consider that they also mean to make people less materialistic.

No matter how much you seek worldly success or think only in a worldly way, for example, "Everything will go well as long as I succeed in this," it may all crumble with a single flood, earthquake, volcanic eruption, or pandemic. Thus, in a sense, I think events like these have a positive side to them.

Medical science was becoming a type of faith, but now it has become clear that medical science cannot cure everything. Even if you get hospitalized for COVID, the most that medical science can offer you is to put you on a ventilator. Doctors are battling to slightly extend their patients' lives, but they should clearly admit that they cannot cure the infection.

Take the case of a flood. If you are hit with a great flood that is described as something you would only see once in several hundred years or a thousand years, then that would be the end for you. There would be nothing you could do. Crops and houses will be ruined, and cars will be washed away. These things will happen, and you will feel helpless.

But even amidst a situation like this, you must reflect on yourself again and humbly restart your life. And when you restart your life, if you can only work on a few things, what will you choose? It is crucial that you choose the important things.

I have titled this chapter, "Follow Your Silent Voice." It means that unless you have a peaceful mind, keep your distance from other people, and make time to look within your mind, you will not gain wisdom.

When I was around 10 years old, I would leave my parents' house at night to study alone. I was alone during my university days, and I was alone when I went abroad for work. I had time to contemplate in silence for about 20 years. What made me different from others is that I often thought and studied on my own and had all kinds of ideas.

Further, although ideas promote work, ideas without inspiration do not have much value. In short, ideas without heavenly inspiration are of little value, let alone those with hellish inspiration.

Simply becoming "empty" at zen temples is not everything. Through meditation, you must be able to receive rightful guidance from the Real World. Sometimes your guardian spirit will not be able to give you enough inspiration, so you must be able to receive guidance from spirits higher than your guardian spirit—namely, the guiding spirits of Happy Science. That will be of great value.

'Now is the time to cultivate your inner mind. I would like you to reconsider various things from this standpoint.

# CHAPTER TWO

# The Road to Cultivate Yourself

## —Speaking on the essence of an intellectual life

Originally recorded in Japanese on September 16, 2021,
at the Special Lecture Hall of Happy Science in Japan
and later translated into English.

# 1

## Preaching the Way of Life That You Should Know Now

### What you should learn to live in society as a human being

In this chapter, I will be going back to the basics, which may be called religion or the study of life. I would like to cover what people should learn before they go out into society.

Since the movie *The Laws of the Universe-The Age of Elohim* (released in 2021, executive producer and original story by Ryuho Okawa) was released (at the time of this lecture), many people have been interested in talks about outer space and are studying it. I do think this is important. Also, our main book for 2022, *The Laws Of Messiah*, has been published. Since this is a teaching that people rarely have

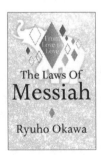

*The Laws Of Messiah*
(New York: IRH Press, 2022)

the chance to read or listen to, it will be an important and precious book for them.

However, here is what I am a little concerned about. Both the laws of the universe and *The Laws Of Messiah* are important and precious, but if you are not careful, you will forget about improving your character, making your life better, or benefiting society. Your mind will instead take a trip to a different world.

Unfortunately, none of you will become a messiah by reading the book, and even if you study the laws of the universe, you will not truly understand the universe. It is OK to learn about those things as part of your knowledge, but what the vast majority of people need are the laws of the bodhisattva.

## Self-centered and conceited people cannot become a bodhisattva

The laws of the bodhisattva are, in Happy Science terms, the laws of the seventh dimension. The seventh dimension is a world where people who can live to help others go. It is a place where such spiritual beings are; many spirits of this dimension are born into this world, and they walk the path of helping others through various occupations.

However, an increasing number of spirits from the Bodhisattva Realm are unable to return to the realm they came from because they lived an easy life on earth or lived a happy-go-lucky life owing to the convenience of this world.

Therefore, it is important to go back to the basics from time to time and look at where you stand. Many young people (at Happy Science), in particular, have a state of mind that belongs to the lower level of the sixth dimension— more precisely, the rear side rather than the front side. In the rear side of the sixth dimension are many *tengu* (long-nosed goblins), *sennin* (hermits), and *yokai*. Despite their mind being at such a level, many of them tend to think they are from the upper level of the eighth dimension or the Sun Realm or maybe even from the ninth dimension. That is why I feel that I must advise them to always look within themselves and look at where they stand now. I feel that many people have become too easy on themselves.

In the sixth dimension, many spirits are working hard to establish themselves, but those who understand the purpose that they are developing themselves for can go up to the Bodhisattva Realm.

Now, what would happen if they worked hard to develop themselves but did nothing more than that? In a worldly sense, they may be called a researcher or a specialist and be able to live their own life to the fullest. However, those people will not reach the level where they live to help others. I would like you to know this distinct difference very well.

Recently, I have been teaching people in different ways not to be self-centered or conceited. People who are highly egoistic or very conceited will not be able to enter the Bodhisattva Realm.

Fundamentally, there are spirits who enter the sixth dimensional world by developing their talents and skills to the fullest, but if they enter the rear side rather than the front side, they will become sennin, tengu, or yokai. So please be careful of this.

# 2

# It Is Difficult to Earn Credibility When You Are Young

## Poems and novels that
## I could not publish during my youth

In 2021, after publishing several books containing my poems, I published a few writings that I had written when I was a student. The manuscripts were found, so I published them as part of the commemoration for the anniversary year of Happy Science.

For example, I published a novel titled *Sareyo, Sareyo, Kanashimi no Shirabe yo* (lit. "Go Away, Go Away, Sad Melodies"). Also, the diary that I wrote from my junior high to university years was compiled into the *Jinsei Note* (lit. "Diary of My Life"). And I recently published *Seishun Tanpen Sakuhin syu: Genjitsu, Musou, soshite Idea no Sekai e* (lit. "Short Stories of My Youth: Reality, Dream, and into the World of Ideas"). I wrote some of the writings when I was around 15 years old, and others I wrote when I was around 20 or 21, during my years at the University of Tokyo, College of Arts and Sciences. So they are not as profound as my books now.

Nevertheless, I would like people to know that even if I did try to publish them back when I was writing them, it would rarely have been allowed. I wrote these things when I was in my teens and in my early 20s. The content has not changed since then, so it would mean that the value of these writings has not changed. Therefore, if these things had been published when I was young, maybe I would have been told that I had great talent and would have been received well by others. In fact, we sometimes see people who become famous while they are young. Some young writers win various "Rookie of the Year" awards and are able to make their debut as a writer. I think this is a wonderful thing.

However, even if the content of a book is valuable, it may not be published if it was written by a young author. Why is that? It is because if a book is published, it will mean that the publishing company has given credibility to the author—putting trust in his or her potential as an author.

Whether it be a newspaper company, a television station, or a publishing company, for example, if a powerful publisher publishes the manuscript of a teen or young adult, it gives them credibility. But even if a young author has their book published, in many cases, 10 years later, when he is 30 years old, he will no longer be writing anything and instead be working a part-time job at something like a convenience store from time to time.

In reality, many people are writing novels as they continue to work part-time at convenience stores. Writers usually go through a "training period" like this. They work part-time jobs to gain various kinds of experience as they draw pictures, make music, sing songs, write novels, or write poems. They have a period of training like this. During this time, they may develop some sort of channel. They may make connections with people or be given a chance to showcase their abilities. Some of them may be able to meet an important person by coincidence.

Imagine that you are good at singing. Even so, there are plenty of others who can sing well, too. You may go to karaoke and show off your singing skills, but it would be very unlikely for someone to overhear you from the room next door and offer you a chance to debut as a singer. If you are working at a company, the most you can expect is to be praised by your colleagues that you are a good singer. So there is quite a long road for such people to become a professional.

## The difficulties of making a living from writing poems

Some people whose poems are used in school textbooks for literature classes actually wrote their poems in their teens or 20s, before they turned 30. I used to carefully read their profiles and saw that many poets died before they were 30, which made me feel that this line of work came with a big trade-off. They burned out like a sparkler. They were able to publish something when they were rich in sensibility, but many of them died when they were roughly 30. Some even committed suicide. A poet's sensibility dries up over time.

Therefore, it is very rare for a person to make a living as a poet. In most cases, they have another job. For example, some people successfully become university professors and write poems while getting paid as a professor. They are very lucky. Back when I was a student, a man named Makoto Ooka was writing *Ori Ori no Uta* (lit. "Poems from Time to Time") in a newspaper column. He wrote poems and described himself as a poet, but because he was also a university professor, the words he used in his poems were very difficult to understand. It may sound rather arrogant for me to say this, but the poems he wrote could not be called poetry. I am not too sure whether he was a professor at the time or how old he was, but that was what I felt when I was 20 years old or so. He used various words in his poems, such as complex terms and Chinese words that he had studied really hard for. However, his poems were not poetry. Instead, I felt that he was in a world of self-satisfaction.

Nonetheless, people whose social status is recognized or who have already made achievements writing books or giving lectures over decades can have their works printed. But whether their works can be deemed "good" is an open question. In fact, those who wrote excellent poems tended to die without being able to make poetry their career. Knowing this, I thought being a poet was a testing job. That is why I truly thought countless times that it is difficult to make a living.

## Why I decided to publish the poems and novels I wrote as a student

When I was young, I thought about these matters very seriously. I wanted to write books and give talks in front of an audience. However, when I thought about whether I could continue these things as a career, make a living, or provide for my family, I asked myself how much credibility I would be given, and I had a negative feeling—I thought it would be impossible. It might have been OK if it were a hobby, but I understood very well that it would not be easy to establish myself as a professional through those things.

Now, after several decades, I am able to publish a collection of poems I wrote during my youth. Many people are interested in the poems I wrote in my younger days and purchase the books because I have already accumulated tons of achievements since graduating from university. In any event, I do not plan to make a living out of these poems, so it will not affect me whether they sell or not or whether the poems are highly or poorly evaluated. I have been successful in my main field, and I have confidence as a professional in my field, so it will not bother me much if people criticize me for my work in other fields.

With this in mind, I have published poems, novels, songs, *haiku*, and *tanka* (*haiku* and *tanka* are short Japanese poems). These were mostly written in my third and fourth years at the University of Tokyo, and some were written in my second year. Back in those days, I could not find a publisher who would publish my work to the world.

Some people may be interested in reading haiku, tanka, poems, or novels written by a religious leader who has given many lectures and written many books. They can read my works and see another side of me—the part of me that is not giving lectures as a religious leader. It means I am developing a new market and creating new customer demand.

However, I must say that this is embarrassing for me. I am already in my 60s but am publishing works that I wrote from age 12 to well into my 20s. I feel a bit uneasy about whether it is OK to publish things that I wrote in my junior high school years. I am also a bit embarrassed about publishing things written in my high school years.

The novel I previously mentioned, *Sareyo, Sareyo, Kanashimi no Shirabe yo*, is a story that I wrote in my second year of university. That is the main content of the book, and as an extra chapter, I added something that I wrote in my second year in high school, on which I based the story.

I did not show this novel to my friends when I was writing it because I knew they would make fun of me. What I have now published after 45 years are the "forgotten works" that were written on manuscript paper and in notebooks.

Most of my poems were also like this. I had a notebook that was imprinted with "Kawashima Junior High School," and the poems I wrote in it were published as a book. I am not sure whether it was really acceptable to publish it, though. People must go through times of trial—a trial to go through embarrassment.

Nonetheless, I believe there is significance in knowing the other talents or reading the past works of a person who has already excelled in a certain field.

## *The Laws of the Sun* was rejected because of my age

I published a series of spiritual message books before resigning from the trading company that I used to work for. When the first spiritual message book was published, I believe I was not even 30. After publishing eight books, I wrote *The Laws of the Sun* (See p. 187) using 300 pages of manuscript paper. At that time, tens of thousands of copies of my spiritual message books had been sold, and I was gaining a certain level of credibility with the company that published those books. However, when I sent in the manuscript of *The Laws of the Sun*, the company left it untouched for three months. I would understand if it was my first book with the company, but the company was already printing 8,000 copies of my spiritual message books in their first printing. Printing 8,000 copies in the first printing was an incredible feat for a small publishing company; usually, the first printing of books is capped at 3,000 copies, and many do not go for additional printing. It was considered a big deal when additional printings sometimes happened.

As for me, I was publishing 8,000 copies and printed an additional 2,000 copies or so several times, which was something that had never happened before at the publishing company. The small publisher was printing one-third-page ads in national newspapers such as *Mainichi Shimbun*, which was something they had never done before; nevertheless, they were able to make enough profit. That is how well the publisher was doing.

Going back to my experience with *The Laws of the Sun*, I wrote it and thought it would sell a million copies, so I sent it to the publisher. However, it was left untouched for three months. When I called the publisher to ask how it was progressing, they told me, "What the author writes has no value, but what the spirits say has value." They kept telling me how there is value in what the higher spirits say but no value in what a living person says. They said that no one would read a book written by a young, 30-year-old man. That really aggravated me. I thought they should read it first before telling me things like that. They did not even read it.

Further, the early spiritual messages we published had my father's name printed in large font, whereas my introduction was printed in small-sized font and in only about three lines. I wondered why they printed my name in such small font. The books that were published under my father's name were all like that. But even in the books of spiritual messages published under my name, my profile was printed at the very bottom, in small-sized letters, and was only three lines long, as if the publisher was ashamed to publish my books. So I asked the publisher, "There must've been something wrong with the printing. Shouldn't the author's profile be printed larger and more boldly?" But the reply I received was, "No, because publishing a book written by a young man without any accomplishments would make our credibility as a publishing company waver." The publisher talked about credibility, but the company itself was not very famous. It was only known among the people interested in the spirituality genre you find in bookstores. Even a small publisher like that would print my name in tiny font because it was an embarrassment. That was how things were when we published our books early on.

## Shoichi Watanabe's frustrating experience publishing his first book

Mr. Shoichi Watanabe wrote that writers usually do not want to remember their first publication. In his book, he wrote something like, "People usually have unpleasant memories of being denied and criticized or being told that their books were not even worth the time."

When he was studying abroad in Germany, he was able to publish a book on English grammar, but when he came back to Japan, he was not able to publish the same book. Sophia University (which he graduated from and also worked at) is now being acknowledged as a prestigious university, and many of its students are able to get into a good company after they graduate. However, back in Mr. Watanabe's days, the university was quite behind the level of Waseda University and Keio University. He was told that people would not buy an English grammar book by a teacher at Sophia University. It meant that teachers at the University of Tokyo and the Tokyo University of Foreign Studies were usually the ones who could publish books about English and that people would not buy a book on English grammar from an English teacher of a not-so-elite school. Even when he brought his book to publishing companies such as *Kenkyusha* and *Gakken*, he was turned down. In the end, he split the cost of publishing in half with the publishing company. After all this, his first book was finally published.

In Germany, Mr. Watanabe attained a doctorate in two years or so and published a book in his mid-20s. However, he had trouble publishing it in Japan. He must have been very frustrated. I, too, have experienced this.

I believe there are many young members at Happy Science. Among them, some may be outstanding in school and perhaps even after graduation but may not be taken seriously by society. Although they might be frustrated by that, it does not mean they are not talented. From the perspective of the companies that are publishing books written by influential and famous people, it is quite a risk to give credibility to a young author. If the author were to cause trouble later on, the publisher would be told by other publishers or authors that they have poor judgment.

Furthermore, writers get very jealous of each other. For instance, there was the late Akiyuki Nosaka, who won the Naoki Prize (a prestigious Japanese award for the best work of popular literature). When Happy Science protested against the content of articles in *Friday* magazine in 1991, he wrote insults and slander about me that were quite troublesome to deal with. However, in the end, he was asking himself whether he did those things because he was jealous of me.

As for me, I never imagined that a Naoki Prize winner would be jealous of me. I was only publishing books because I felt it was necessary to continue spreading the Truth that our religion taught.

## You need to know the "common sense" of the industry

Happy Science's publishing company, IRH Press, was quite bold. For example, when we published *The Terrifying Revelations of Nostradamus* (1991), which was later made into a movie, IRH Press placed an ad in the newspaper that said, "700,000 copies, first printing." This was not a lie. We really did print 700,000 copies of *The Terrifying Revelations of Nostradamus* in its first printing. We also printed 300,000 copies of *The Great Warning of Allah* in its first printing. IRH Press was not very experienced as a publishing company, so it really did print that many copies. We did not understand why everyone usually printed a small number of copies to start with and then printed additional copies when the book sold well. We had almost no idea that unsold books would be returned.

In those days, there was an executive staff member of Happy Science who had previously worked at a company that published a magazine called *Reader's Digest*. When I had him work for IRH Press, he printed the slogan, "An astonishing return rate of 12 percent," on the company envelope. I told him, "Why on earth would you write such an embarrassing catchphrase?! Obviously, our return rate should be zero percent. Do you think that writing 12 percent is a good advertising line?!"

However, the number was, in fact, outstanding. Usually, unsold books are returned within 3-4 days. Books are displayed at bookstores, but if they do not sell, they are immediately returned. Hundreds of new books come out every day, so if the books displayed in bookstores do not sell, bookstores must return those books and display new ones. Otherwise, it would be similar to a fish shop selling rotten fish. To display 100 or 200 new books, bookstores need to make space for them, so they must return the books they feel will not sell. If bookstores return those books, they will not have to pay, but the publishers will already have paid for the cost of printing and might also have to pay for royalties.

This is why the first publishing company I worked with sent me a publishing contract for my first spiritual message but not again after that. The reason is that if a publisher signs a contract, it will have to pay me even if my books do not sell. The publisher told me it was the same whether we both signed the contract or not and did not send me the contract, no matter how many times I asked. In truth, the publishing company probably thought that if my books sold, they would pay me royalties, but if the books did not sell and were returned, they would try to avoid paying me by postponing or only paying a portion of the royalties. Many other writers must have experienced this.

Here is an episode from a time I visited the publishing company that was publishing my books. As I walked in, I had to weave my way through a path flanked by mountains of returned books. Publishing companies stack returned books in that way so that writers would not be able to tell them, "Sell more copies" or "Pay the royalties." The publisher I worked with made sure that it was clear to the writer that there were lots of returned books.

Fortunately, most of my books were not returned; instead, additional copies were printed again and again. The first print run would be 8,000 copies, followed by additional print runs, again and again, up to 15,000 or 20,000 copies. But I already had in my mind that they would sell a bit more than that from the very beginning. However, when I heard various stories about the publishing industry, I realized that publishers are looking for books that will sell 10,000 copies. They are frantically looking with the utmost effort to see which books will sell 10,000 copies. You would not understand this if you did not know what is considered common sense in the publishing world.

## In society, you will not be recognized for your talent alone

That is how the writings of a 30-year-old are treated. The point is, even though I had published eight or nine books of spiritual messages and had sold well over 100,000 copies in total, the manuscript of *The Laws of the Sun*, a book I wrote in my own words and which eventually sold millions of copies through IRH Press, was not even read by the publishing company. I would like you to know about this.

I was not without achievements. Even so, a book about my own enlightenment, not a spiritual message, was put aside. The publisher felt that this kind of content could be published only by an older leading figure, and that although a writer at 60 may be respectable, a writer at 50 is not old enough to be trusted.

I am saying that it takes years or decades to see what becomes of a person. If you look at their past and their achievements, you will understand what kind of person they are. However, if you believe that the person is talented and risk it on their talents alone, it would be like betting on a racehorse. It is a truly risky gamble.

Some people may look at someone's painting and say, "This person has a lot of talent. Let's make him a professional painter." Some people may listen to a song that someone makes or sings and say, "This person is talented, so let's promote them" or "Let's sell their single album." Happy Science has a tendency to do this, but we can do such things because we have a surplus in other areas of management. In this way, when we see that someone has talent, we give the person an opportunity to sell themselves. But that is not how things usually work in society because people think about collecting on their expenses. They look for people who have already made achievements.

Of course, there are skillful music talent scouts. People with a keen eye for talent travel across the country to see people holding live concerts at a small venue or a free venue or performing on the streets and pick out those they think will be successful. However, many of them fail after one song. Please know that this is the usual case in life.

## What to keep in mind if you are unsatisfied with the way you are treated

There are students who endlessly complain about how people treat them because they are not acknowledged despite their skills. I believe some students who graduated from university in the last few years are saying, "I can do a lot, but they treat me so poorly at work." People who think they were highly capable in school may have gotten straight A's or a high GPA, or they may have perhaps completed a famous seminar course taught at a highly prestigious school. Others may have been proficient in English skills and have passed the highest level of the EIKEN (Test in Practical English Proficiency) or gained a perfect score of 990 on the TOEIC test. These may all look good on a resume.

I heard that some people quit their jobs after three months, saying, "I have a TOEIC score of 990, yet they only let me answer incoming phone calls. This is a black company (a company with poor working conditions), so I will quit!"

However, you must understand that you will not even be able to properly answer phone calls. Even if you scored 990 on the TOEIC test, you would not know who is calling your company, so you will not be able to answer phone calls. This is because you will not understand what the other person is saying. If you do not know everything that the company does, you will not understand what the caller is referring to or know what the caller is complaining about. So you just have to accept things as they are.

Let me give you another example. Say that a university student graduated with excellent grades and got into the Ministry of Finance. His work for the first two years will just be to photocopy documents. On average, new hires like him will make about 100,000 copies. Then, after two years, they will start visiting the opposition parties to obtain the questions that will be asked at national diet sessions and attach papers with the answers to those questions.

A famous female lawyer sold herself by saying she graduated with straight A's. Before becoming a lawyer, she worked at the Ministry of Finance, photocopying and cutting out newspaper articles. The Ministry of Finance had subscribed to five different newspapers, and she cut out the articles pertaining to the ministry and filed them. Her job was just filing articles. But most of the time, her superior did not even bother to look at those articles. She was made to do this kind of work.

Then, she quit after two years and went to the Legal Research and Training Institute to become a lawyer. But after working as a lawyer for a while, she quit, went to study abroad in the United States, and came back with straight A's. Ultimately, she became an associate professor at a university.

In general, large businesses in Japan actually give you trivial work to do. Many people may simply do nothing more than photocopying. However, the important thing is for you to read and understand what kind of documents you are copying. You must know this very well. Whether someone will do this depends on whether they have an appetite for learning. The point here is to figure out the subject of concern. You must look at the topics being covered in the document and be able to read them before you bring the copies to your superiors. In short, you must understand what kind of work is being done.

The same can be said about answering phone calls. People call your workplace about all kinds of work, including work that does not directly involve you, but you must come to understand what kind of work other people are doing by answering the calls. If you respond by saying, "I was assigned to this task only, so other tasks have nothing to do with me," you will most likely lose customers.

Let me introduce a case that occurred at Happy Science. When we opened our first branch, which was the Kansai Branch, the staff there was taking phone calls. I will not reveal his name because he is currently working hard as the head of a shoja, but back then, he would always answer the phone in the same way, so people thought his voice was an answering machine greeting. He would say, "Hello, this is Happy Science Kansai Temple," but many people thought it was an answering machine and hung up on him. It was as if we were paying him to sit there and reduce the number of our members. He is now doing well as the head of a shoja, so I believe he has changed, but at that time, many people thought his answers to calls were like a monotonous answering machine. Therefore, you must think about the purpose of your job.

## People will not acknowledge you
## unless you are experienced, old, and accomplished

This may be hard for young people to accept, but you are not being told that you do not have talent. To fully let your talents flourish, you must be experienced enough, old enough, and accomplished enough. Otherwise, people will not acknowledge you. This is a difficult matter. It is a very, very difficult issue.

I had a similar experience when I self-published the pamphlet of poems, *Love for God: from its beginning*. I paid ¥300,000 to print 100 copies and handed them out to people I knew. Also, I forgot which company I specifically sent it to, but I do remember receiving no response when I sent it to a publishing company that often published poems. That is how the world works.

People will go to a fishing spot if they have been able to catch a lot of fish there, but as for a new spot, they will not bother fishing there if they do not know whether they will catch anything. Likewise, people do not bother reading something that is unpredictable.

The same goes for manga. Although I do not read them much now, I used to read them when I was in elementary school. I once watched a movie about young manga artists, and it was truly astounding. It was an interesting world. The editors read through the pages with tremendous speed the first time. Manga editors, in general, are seeing whether the manga is at a level worthy of further inspection, and if they deem it not to be, they tell you to go home. If they skim through it the first time and feel that there is something special about it, then they will read the story more thoroughly.

Specialists are all like that; they make a judgment right then and there. Usually, these quick judgments are negative. If something is no-good, they tell you right away. On the other hand, they will not easily say something is good work because saying it is good comes with heavy responsibilities. You must know this. If you misinterpret this, you may suffer dire consequences.

# 3

# The Key to Becoming a Professional— Managing Time and Reading Books

## The time I spent writing the novel
### *Chikyu Mangekyo*

From July to August 2021, I handwrote a novel on paper titled *Chikyu Mangekyo* (Earth Kaleidoscope). I believe it has been 30 years, perhaps even longer, since I last wrote something like that.

Usually, the lectures I give are typed and compiled into a book, so from the standpoint of time efficiency, writing books by hand is unproductive for me. For example, if I were to make a book of this size (holds up *Chikyu Mangekyo*), I would not need to give a lecture of two hours. So if I talk for an hour and 15 minutes, I can make a book of this size and publish it as it is.

Now, how long did it take me to handwrite this when I could have spoken the same amount of words in 75 minutes? About two weeks. But I was not writing it all day long. I wrote for an hour in the evening and an hour in the morning, so it took about 30 hours in total for me to write it. I spent 30 hours writing what I could have spoken in 75 minutes, which means it was a very inefficient use of time. So the fact that

I handwrote it meant I was very conscious about including added value in the novel.

It is true that handwritten sentences are pithy and do not have excess content. Also, I am able to edit and revise my writing by polishing my sentences and choosing my words. In this way, oftentimes, the sentences look better. However, if I am going to publish something like this, I must look at it from the standpoint of time management and decide whether I really should spend time doing it.

I had a rough idea of how much work I needed to do in the summer of 2021, but I finished most of it before the Celebration of Lord El Cantare's Descent (held on July 11). I had some time to spare, so I thought I would write a simple novel. That is how I came to write *Chikyu Mangekyo*.

If you wish to become a professional, it comes down to how you use your time. This applies to everything. As I have said many times before, humans have 24 hours in a day. Within these 24 hours, you also need time for daily activities and sleep, so in reality, you do not have much time for work. Usually, you can spend about eight hours doing work.

Nevertheless, if you are working toward writing things or releasing information, then you need time to gather sources as well as time to polish and deepen your thoughts. It is not like farming, where each stroke of the plow will immediately influence your work. Instead, it is like rice; you plant seedlings in the spring and harvest them in the autumn. So it is very difficult to consider the time you spend gathering, brewing, or fermenting ideas a part of your work. If the time you spend doing such things does not produce any fruits or any results, then it could end up being a waste of time. This is the truly difficult part.

## Are you efficiently reading books?

If you are trying to do a good job or trying to become a respectable person, then the basic attitude to have is to be smart about how you read books. There are many tools of learning available now, but it would be hard to say that just watching TV for long hours will make someone a cultivated person. Sometimes, NHK Educational TV airs informative programs, and perhaps you will become knowledgeable about history by watching them. But if you were to give a lecture or write something, watching TV is not enough.

Moreover, in the current age of the internet, the quality of information has drastically fallen, but the quantity of information has tremendously increased, so you are more than likely to waste time. If you plan on spending time doing something, you should use it on a high-quality activity. Otherwise, you are losing out. In that sense, newspaper companies and TV stations go through one or two levels of review before they release news. They are trying to decrease the amount of unimportant information before releasing it to the public.

As for books, many of the long-selling books or classics that are still being read even after hundreds, a thousand, or two thousand years have already established a good reputation. You will not lose out by reading them. Therefore, if you are going to use the same amount of time, it would be a waste if you use it on something that does not have high-quality content.

However, you often need to concentrate more when you read books that are difficult or full of content, so you will tend to read things that are easier. In short, you will read books that are lighter in content. Some of you might even think that reading text is a hassle and instead watch videos, whereas others may be satisfied with just reading magazines.

Of course, magazine editors may need to know a wide variety of trivia, so they will need to read all kinds of information. However, if you wish to be appropriately acknowledged, you must develop a method of studying that allows you to efficiently absorb high-quality information. There is no other way.

Nowadays, I read many books; people might misunderstand this, but the basis of studying is to intensively and meticulously read books. Reading books will mean nothing if you have not built this foundation; there is no good in reading books in the same way you skim through comic books. If you do not understand this and are just skimming through different information, then nothing will "crystallize." If there is no core, nothing will crystallize.

You may feel it is not enough to just meticulously study a certain topic and therefore decide to gather other materials or find something that will give you a hint. In doing so, you may come across things that are useful or that can serve as a hint. However, if you only look for these types of things, you will ultimately be reading through heaps of garbage or piles of dust; thus, you will not succeed in anything.

# 4

# A Cultivated Person Balances Intensive Reading with Extensive Reading

## Intensive reading starts with careful study for entrance exams

As a student, I read quite a lot of books and did a considerable amount of intensive reading in particular. My intensive reading skill fundamentally comes from the way I studied for entrance exams. In Japan, elementary, junior high, and high school students may take entrance exams. Those who have slacked off and not studied thoroughly for those exams will often have trouble later on. They will have to make up for it at some point; otherwise, they will have a hard time in the future. Those who have intensively read and studied hard can become cultivated people by building on that foundation. Those who slack off will have to go through a lot of training and self-study.

Think about it. Whether it be junior high or high school, textbooks for Contemporary Japanese classes have excerpts of work written by various authors, and teachers cover them in the span of a year or perhaps six months. These classes basically focus on intensive reading.

Therefore, if you want to do well on the midterm or final exam in Contemporary Japanese, it would be wise for you to thoroughly read the areas you will be tested on. To put it simply, you must look up the words or phrases you do not know in the dictionary and think about how the sentences are phrased, how punctuation is used, and what the sentences are trying to tell you. Speaking from my experience, after I read the passages five times with such a mindset, I was able to get a perfect score on high school Contemporary Japanese exams.

The people writing the exam questions are at that level. For example, there are excerpts from novels in Contemporary Japanese textbooks, so you must think, "If I were to make test questions out of this excerpt, what would I ask?" As you look up vocabulary you do not know and read the passage a few times, you will realize which parts are difficult for people to understand. There are parts in a passage that will be misread or overlooked if they are read only once. In most cases, people make trick questions based on those parts, or they make you explain them. Thus, if you meticulously read the text five times, you will be able to get a perfect score. This is absolutely true. So you need to develop a detail-oriented brain.

What will happen if you do not make an effort to do this but instead just read the text without comprehending it? You can likely find some novelists who are high school dropouts. Conversely, although many people drop out of school, it does not mean that they will become novelists. I do not necessarily think that dropping out of school is the shortcut to becoming a novelist. Some people are always reading books and do not bother going to school; out of those people, a few may become novelists or writers, but it is very unlikely.

Nowadays, people who are trying to become writers take on some kind of day job because they are not acknowledged right away. They work to get a paycheck every month and write during their days off or at night. Then, they might have their work printed or might win an award, and they might even be offered a writing job. That is how writers start out. For this reason, it is wiser to first train yourself so you are able to get a job.

## Keep working on yourself until your talent blooms

Only a few talented people can make a living using their talent.

Let me talk about Sota Fujii, a Japanese professional shogi (Japanese chess) player ranked 9-dan. He dropped out of high school one month before graduation because he already knew that he could make a living off of shogi. If he had continued going to school, he would have had less time to spend studying shogi. Many people would challenge him, so he needed to study their past shogi matches. It makes a tremendous difference whether you have studied all of an opponent's past shogi matches or not. Knowing how your opponent plays allows you to come up with strategies that will increase your probability of winning. Conversely, not knowing your opponent's playing style will reduce your chance of winning. That is why he dropped out of school. But because he can make a living off of it, it is OK.

There are millions of, if not 10 million, shogi players overall, but the probability of someone becoming a professional like Fujii is one in a million. The first opponent Fujii faced as a professional shogi player was former *meijin* (one of the most prestigious shogi titles) Hifumi Kato, and Kato lost. A few months later, Kato retired, possibly thinking that his career was over since he lost to a junior high schooler who was 4-dan. He probably did not know that Fujii was so strong. Sometime after that, Fujii also won against Yoshiharu Habu, who used to be a seven-title holder. If Kato knew Fujii could defeat Habu, he might not have retired. It is hard to believe, but if you happen to go against a person with talent that is one in a million, the unexpected can happen.

However, in general, you should take an orthodox approach—continue to study for exams and work hard so you can get a job. A glimmer of your talent will show during your teens and 20s. Other people may not notice it, or sometimes they may tell you about your talent. In some cases, you may notice your own talent, but when you do, you might have a skewed view of it, or you might realize it a little late. Or perhaps people with keen eyes will discover your talent.

So it is best for you to remember your talent and keep working on yourself until your talent blooms.

## As a student, I had my thoughts printed on paper on two occasions

Here is an episode where my work was printed outside of school. The first time my work was printed on paper was when I was in my third year of junior high school (equivalent to ninth grade in the United States). It was either in the monthly magazine called *Chu San Course* (lit. "Ninth Grade Course") or *Chu Ni Course* ("Eighth Grade Course") that was published by Gakken Holdings, Ltd. Although I was in ninth grade, what I said at that time might have been printed in the eighth grade magazine. I do not exactly remember, but I am quite sure it was published shortly after summer vacation. The title was something like, "My Three-Step Study Method," but in truth, I did not write it myself. I took part in a phone interview from Tokyo during lunchtime at school, and the person working at Gakken summarized the content into the "three-step study method." The title was something they came up with, and they included my photo and my profile. I was quite surprised as to how much they could write without actually seeing me face to face. All I did was answer questions in a phone interview, but they were able to write an article about me, including things such as, "He is warmhearted." I was surprised to know that they could write this and learned that this is how magazine articles are written. It was printed on paper, and a crowd of students gathered to read it in the library. This was my first experience with having my thoughts printed outside of school.

Another episode is from the year I entered university. A comment I sent to *Asahi Shimbun*, a quality newspaper in Japan, was printed in its "letters to the editor" column. However, this experience was a bit embarrassing. Back then, many students read *Asahi Shimbun*, and many of them would say things about it when I walked around campus. It was truly embarrassing. Some would tell me, "Hey, I saw it!" or "I read it," whereas others who had not read the article but heard about it said, "I heard you won the Akutagawa Prize (the most prestigious award for new writers)." I, myself, was thinking, "Please give me a break." I wrote something that went against conventional thinking, and they published a counterargument a little later. That is how I learned to write sentences that can be printed in a newspaper.

## Translating "Vox Populi, Vox Dei" from Japanese to English and vice versa helped me later on

Let me introduce a story I wrote in my books such as *Eigo ga Hiraku Jinseiron, Shigotoron* (lit. "English Opens a Path in Your Life and Work") and *Benkyou no Kotsu* ("Tips for Studying"). It was about something I did from the end of my second year in high school until the summer vacation of my third year. I would cut out the column, "Vox Populi, Vox Dei" of *Asahi Shimbun* and see if I could translate the Japanese sentences into English. The English translations were printed in *Asahi Evening News* the next day. When the English translations came out, I would see if I could translate them into Japanese. However, it was quite difficult to come up with the same level of Japanese as the person writing "Vox Populi, Vox Dei." My notebook grew twice as thick after many days of translating Japanese sentences into English and vice versa, as well as cutting out and pasting the "Vox Populi, Vox Dei" columns on both sides. Looking back, I was filled with nostalgia, thinking about how much I had done. But in reality, I felt that the more I did those things, the less intelligent I became. Even though I thought of it as a high level of studying, I was doing worse in my English class.

Actually, my English teacher was the one who recommended I read the "Vox Populi, Vox Dei" column.

He told me, "Once everyone gets to the top of the class, they want to study something harder than the level they are studying for the entrance exams. So they start reading English newspapers or magazines such as *Newsweek* or *TIME*. The top-level students are all like that, so just studying what you learn in school is not enough."

He was also my homeroom teacher, and I went along with his advice, but my grades went down. Ironically, the conclusion was simple: If I had worked on the reference material assigned by the school over and over, my grades would have gone up. Other students who did this were able to keep their high grades in English class. On the contrary, I, who was practicing translation with the "Vox Populi, Vox Dei" column, was the one suffering in English class. I remember feeling how strange it was because what I was doing was a high level of study.

But this practice ultimately had positive effects after I graduated from university. An average Japanese person cannot write essays in English. Even if they are very skilled in English, they cannot write essays in English. However, in my case, I was able to do so. I wondered why and realized that it was thanks to my year-long training of consistently translating "Vox Populi, Vox Dei" articles. Each of my translations came out to about 2-3 pages long on manuscript paper—or 800-1,200 characters.

The Japanese sentences written in the column were excellent, so I practiced how I could translate them into English and translate the English sentences printed in *Asahi Evening News* into excellent Japanese sentences. Although the practice lowered my grades, it had a positive effect later on.

## What I said shocked my professor at the university

After reading my novels, I was able to reconfirm the fact that I was reading books in their original English text during my time in the College of Arts and Sciences, which means during my first and second year of university (refer to the aforementioned *Sareyo, Sareyo, Kanashimi no Shirabe yo, Jinsei Note*, and *Seishun Tanpen Sakuhin syu: Genjitsu, Musou, soshite Idea no Sekai e*). These novels were not scheduled to be published, so what is written there is not made up. If you read the novels, you will see that I was reading the original English text.

However, at that time, neither the professor nor the assistant professor could easily read books in their original English version, so I was rather shocked. I had thought that it was the norm for professors and assistant professors to read books in their original English text with ease, but I figured out that the professors could not do so during seminar class.

One day, a professor who held a seminar based on the original English text of a book accidentally came to class having read the passage for the next seminar. Therefore, he did not read the part that was to be covered in the lecture on that day. So he asked if he could take some time to read it. He read the passage with the utmost effort, and I saw that it took him as long as 15 minutes, so I understood right away that his English skills were poorer than mine.

Perhaps it is better for you not to accept a student like me into your class. It is probably wise not to have such a sarcastic, bully-like, or rude student in your seminar. You shouldn't keep such an "irritating" student, who times the reading speed of a professor, close to you. I was sitting next to the professor, and it could have looked as though I was the professor. I really was timing my professor's reading speed—testing his skill and counting the words.

For your information, it was not the first time the professor had read the book. The book was used in previous seminars, so he must have read it before. It was just that he had read the wrong passage for the class that day. And when I timed how fast he could read, I found out he read it slower than me and was disappointed.

On another day, I talked with an assistant professor of another class. I was telling him how I was thinking of becoming a political scholar as my future career, and he asked me what I was reading. I told him I was reading

Hannah Arendt as my focus, mainly in English but also in German. Hannah Arendt's English is influenced by German, so I could also read it in German.

Then, he told me that I should not read Hannah Arendt because it was too difficult and asked me whether I was reading other books, such as novels. I answered that I was reading *The Grapes of Wrath* by Steinbeck in English. I remember him being very surprised; he said, "Why are you reading something like that?" But I must say that the book has to do with political science. The book talks in detail about the discrimination people, such as those of Japanese descent, faced in the West Coast of the United States and how they were forced to live in certain regions. So the book has to do with political science. From the book, you can get a better idea of what things were like in the United States before World War II.

Going back to my conversation with the assistant professor, I remember that when I told him I was reading the original English version of *The Grapes of Wrath* by Steinbeck, he seemed to be offended. I asked what he was reading, and he told me he was reading a Japanese novel by Jun Ishikawa. So I asked him, "Is that so? How good is he? Is he that good?" Then, he told me, "What are you saying? There is no good or bad when it comes to novels. It is the reader's preference." I had never heard of the novelist writing good books, so I wondered why the assistant professor was reading his works.

On the one hand, a student reads Steinbeck in English; on the other hand, the assistant professor reads a work by a second-rate novelist in Japanese. Now, would you take a class in International Politics from this assistant professor? Unfortunately, the class was not ready for an "arrogant" student like me.

So I felt that although I was making more effort and had more talent than I expected, I was not heading down a conventional path.

## Balancing both intensive and extensive reading is the path to being a top-level expert

If you look at the way I study, it has elements of a straightforward approach to studying or an orthodox way of studying that a bright student would take, and at the same time, it has elements of self-study. These are the two methods I use. This may be difficult to understand, but I tried to incorporate the orthodox way of studying when it came to things that were my specialty or things that were directly related to my work. For things that were beyond my field of specialty, I set for myself a level of how much I should understand about that field. Of course, I set different levels for sub-specialties and non-specialties and changed my reading speed based on those levels.

Whether you are seeking to become a scholar, a brilliant person, or a competent office worker, you need to be able to read intensively, whether it is in Japanese or some other foreign language. If you are unable to do this, you will often misunderstand the instructions given to you and make many mistakes, or you may even misunderstand a conversation. You will receive instructions but relay them in the wrong way. If you are told many things and are asked to relay the message to someone else, it will not accurately reach the person. If this is the case, it means you tend to skim-read and overlook many important things when you read something. Therefore, it is important to train your brain through studying for entrance exams because it will have a 70–80 percent influence on your work.

However, I must say that it will not be enough on its own to make you a cultivated person. You will most likely be able to get a job that earns you enough salary to support your family, but you will not be able to go beyond that and enter the world to greater success. You must balance both intensive and extensive reading, which is truly difficult to accomplish.

Usually, people who *can* extensively read *cannot* intensively read, and vice versa. So balancing these two ways of reading requires the skill of a genius. You need a different ability to be able to do this. Therefore, only a handful of people can do both types of reading. The number of such capable readers drastically drops.

Some professors at universities who publish only a few books may somehow finish writing a textbook before retirement. These people can intensively read. However, I do not think they can extensively read. People who cannot extensively read cannot do well in the literary world by writing and publishing many books or commenting on things like critics do.

Another way to balance both types of reading is to change the way you read according to your age. For example, you can focus on intensive reading when you are young, and after accumulating considerable knowledge, you can speed up your reading and work on extensive reading. Only those who have managed to balance the two will be able to become top-level experts in their specialized areas and be able to make comments on other fields.

Category-wise, I may be considered a religious professional, but I am able to give my opinion on politics, philosophy, and other areas. I can even compose music or write poems, novels, and other things if I want to. This is because I read and study a wide range of genres.

## It takes willpower to do highly productive work

One thing that allows a person to balance intensive and extensive reading is willpower. Please know that unless you are able to balance the two, your level of productivity will never rise. In this way, those who only study as if studying at school and only have the ability to repeatedly study and master what was written in the workbook or reference material to prepare for a midterm or final exam will not be able to do a higher level of work than the average salaried worker. Unless you also study genres other than what you are directly involved with, you will never be able to do creative work or work that is highly productive compared with an average Joe. If you do not have this different eye, you will not be able to make new discoveries. This part is very difficult, and it requires willpower. You must know this.

Let me give you an example. If you are a religious professional, you do not necessarily need to know history in depth as your field of expertise. However, if you teach religion as a professional, have a hobby of reading historical novels, and read far beyond the number of historical novels an average person reads, you will probably become a religious professional who knows a lot about history. Then, when you give a lecture, the people listening will feel that they have learned something new or useful to them.

Some Buddhist monks undergo spiritual discipline by secluding themselves in the mountain for 10 years. They seclude themselves and study at a place like a temple located on Mt. Hiei. There is food and water, and they sometimes go for a walk in the mountains, but the main point is that they seclude themselves to cut off all information from the secular world. This kind of discipline has existed since long ago.

They do not read newspapers or watch TV to get information. They only recite sutras and do not read or hear information about the secular world for 10 years, so they will most likely turn out to be like Robinson Crusoe. And suppose that after 10 years of holy training, the monk is appointed as the chief monk of a temple. He will not understand what others are saying to him. Perhaps a prisoner would know more than him. In prison, inmates can read anything except for what is blacked out. They can read books or newspapers if they request them, so there is a chance that an inmate who made an effort to study will know more than him. So for monks, being in seclusion could be counterproductive.

It is true that, to focus your mind or meditate for some time and enter the spiritual world, you must shut off secular vibrations. Unless you block out worldly information with beta waves, you will not be able to elevate your mind to the state of arhat.

On the contrary, if you cut yourself off from the secular world too much, you will not be able to do the work of a bodhisattva because you will not understand what is going on in the world. If you lose interest in what is happening in the world or in your country and only read a part of the Tripitaka over and over, one million times, you will not be able to save people, which is the main work of religion.

## Making a habit of using small chunks of time for studying

So far, I have talked about the importance of being able to intensively and extensively read. But to practice both, you need willpower and the power of perseverance to make continuous efforts; you also need to find small chunks of time. What I mean is that you should look for small chunks of time or periods of time that you can use within a certain time frame. For example, this can be the time during your commute to work, or it can refer to your time in the bathroom, in the bathtub, or at a coffee shop. Of course, there could be other periods of time you can use. If you are able to make small but steady efforts, you will be able to get the results you expect.

Another example would be when you are behind the wheel and cannot do anything else. You could listen to something as long as you do not get into a traffic accident. You could listen to popular songs and memorize them. You could even listen to classical music, sutras, or lectures. You have lots of options. What will you pick, and at what time of the day will you do it? That will reflect whether you are smart or not, and the only way to tell this is to wait and see the results. After all, whether you are smart or not is determined by how well or poorly you use time.

Earlier, I mentioned to you the significance of intensive reading, extensive reading, making use of small chunks of time, and the power to make continuous efforts. Now, I would also like to talk about the importance of motivating yourself at certain points in your life.

Many people think, "Because I studied it, I am done with it," but actually, that is not true. Here is a case to consider: Some people are saying that more people are reading now because they are staying at home due to COVID. Not only did the population of people reading increase, but the number of people who read picture books has also increased, and the market for picture books is expanding. This is probably because the adults who are staying at home have more time to read books to their children or because they enjoy reading picture books rather than reading books with a lot of words. Some adults who have read more picture books than average could possibly become picture book connoisseurs. They would be able to tell whether the pictures are of good or bad quality and whether the story is good or not. People could reach a level where they are able to give opinions like this.

Speaking of the importance of making continuous efforts, allow me to bring up the *Kuro-Obi Eigo* (Black Belt English) series that I have been publishing. To date, I have published 120 of these books. If I include the manuscripts that are in the making, this will bring the number up to a total of 130 books. This is a project that I have been working on for 10 years. As you can see, if you continue to work on something every month for 10 years, you will have more than 100 books.

I am neither a professional in English education nor a researcher of English, so in that sense, I do not need to publish these books. However, I believe that it is necessary to create this text for my own learning and for the staff and members of Happy Science to be able to spread the Truth in other countries, so I have made it my habit to produce one book per month.

Sadly, although I can produce one book of *Kuro-Obi Eigo* per month, many people cannot even read one book of the series in a month, which is surprising to me. I do not spend a whole day producing *Kuro-Obi Eigo* books. Rather, I am using small chunks of time each day to prepare the content little by little. I split the work into small increments and use chunks of time to do it, but in total, I do not spend more than 30 minutes a day. I use chunks of five or ten minutes to come up with the content for one book in less than a month.

It takes a month to produce it, yet the readers are not able to read it in a month, which makes me wonder why. I mean, the readers must develop a habit of deciding when and which chunks of time they will use to read it. If you can develop the habit of mechanically doing this, you will be able to read the *Kuro-Obi Eigo* books. The same goes for your studies.

To do something mechanically may seem like a low-level thing to do, but it also applies to highly spiritual work. You will need to be able to do the work mechanically, or you will not be able to do it for long. Please know that making continuous efforts leads to building up power.

# 5

## Make Time to Be Alone and Take an Interest in Society

### It is important for religious professionals to know about people's worries and sufferings

As I mentioned previously, if you choose to isolate yourself at a temple for 10 years, you will have no idea what is going on in the world. As a religious professional, it is also important to know about people's worries and sufferings. When you are young, you are mostly concerned with your own worries and sufferings, but when you start working in religion, you will need to have the knowledge or skill or be able to give advice on how to solve people's worries and sufferings.

Let me give you an example. The collared shirt that I am wearing today may seem like an ordinary shirt from afar, but if you look closely, you will see that it has detailed openwork patterns on it. Only those who look at it from up close will notice; to others, it only looks white. The company that made this shirt was not very large, but it was a good company that did a meticulous and detailed job. That is why I bought their shirts, but I heard yesterday that it went bankrupt because a state of emergency was declared many times. I heard that the company had a debt of ¥50 million.

Politicians are only thinking about saving people who have been infected by COVID. When they are told that many companies have gone bankrupt and could not be saved because of the state of emergency they declared, they shifted the blame and said that the banks had given out loans to those companies before they failed. However, companies are going bankrupt precisely because there are no customers coming in. So it is meaningless for banks to give out loans to those companies.

For instance, if a department store is told to close, its tenants will go bankrupt, of course, because they would not be able to do business. Shops will close down whenever they are pressured by something beyond their capabilities. What do politicians think when they hear this?

These days, people talk about taking countermeasures against COVID, and we often hear or read about the bed occupancy rates of COVID patients or the number of people dying from COVID. News articles mainly talk about hospital beds being full or the health system collapsing, but the reality is that companies are going under for reasons politicians least expected.

Last year, I heard on the news that the owner of a tonkatsu (deep-fried pork cutlet) restaurant in Nerima, Tokyo burned himself to death by pouring frying oil on himself and setting himself on fire. He was the leader of a group of shop owners on a shopping street. Although he graduated from the prestigious Faculty of Economics at Keio University, he ran a tonkatsu restaurant, perhaps because it was a family business. But the COVID-19 recession hit his business, and he poured oil on himself and lit himself on fire, like the Tibetan monks. In short, he probably wanted to protest against the poor policy implemented by the government.

Declaring a state of emergency will ruin tonkatsu shops. I am certain that government officials do not even think about this. They listen to the experts in the medical field and scholars of infectious diseases and do as they say, but those specialists do not understand which businesses will go bankrupt or what will go wrong. So this point needs to be considered.

From a religious professional's point of view, it might not be their main line of work to speak out about economic issues, but if people actually have trouble putting food on the table every day or if they have no choice but to kill themselves, then that is a religious matter. Can we provide another solution to people who try to burn themselves to death? What can we do to prevent shops in a department store from going bankrupt when the department store remains closed? What if a company making collared shirts goes under? Perhaps the company has little to do with the coronavirus. The company's workers take their customers' measurements, but they are not so close to their customers that they would go out drinking with them for a sales talk, so they probably are not so affected by the virus. Anyhow, as I observe many companies closing down, I think to myself, "As a religious professional, I must be alert and remain sensitive to what is going on in the world."

## Being attentive to society's suffering while being detached from society

What are people suffering over now? You must know about it. It means expanding your knowledge on subjects that are not your expertise. You should be perceptive to all kinds of matters. Then, you will begin to see various studies and arts as subjects of religious concern. Even things like how we should design and reform our society and its systems must be considered.

Suppose you are at a cafe, and one of the other customers complains, "There's nothing we can do unless someone comes up with a policy that will improve the economy." Or the cafe manager might tell you, "Customers in their 40s–60s do nothing but complain. They all grumble." In this way, you should listen and learn what is going on in the world.

Therefore, you must intensively and extensively read. Also, you must detach yourself from society to master your field of expertise and, at the same time, know what people are worrying or suffering over when you start helping them as a bodhisattva.

In the novels I wrote in my younger days, you will see that there were many times when I felt I was in solitude. And in those lonely times, although I was spending my days as a student, I believe I was experiencing something that a person at Eiheiji Temple experiences in zen meditation. I was detached from society while living through trifling matters. But I must say, even though I was detached from society, I aspired to study and learn many more things to save the people in the world. It was also important to sometimes motivate myself to do that.

# 6

## You Can Still Grow
## Regardless of Your Age

### Relearning English from age 45

Let me tell you another story regarding English. I used to work for a trading company where people used English, so I also used it until I resigned at the age of 30. In those days, I was studying English, of course, and my daily work consisted of working with documents all written in English. So I was learning English regardless of whether I was consciously doing so. At 30, I became a religious professional, and I did not need to use English for some time. But at 45, I relearned English because I felt my English skills were declining. There was a particular incident that made me realize my English skills were going downhill. I have mentioned this a few times before.

When one of my children was attending a prestigious junior high school, we had a tutor who was a graduate of Waseda University, School of Political Science and Economics. He could not solve my daughter's English test—it was a test on English conversation in a fill-in-the-blank format. He did not know what to write in the blanks. I was quite disappointed to find out that a graduate of Waseda

University, School of Political Science and Economics, could not solve an eighth-grader's English assignment. Let's hope he is not working in a key position at Happy Science.

The tutor told her, "I don't know the answer. Please ask your father." That was not very nice of him. Even though I was busy, he told her, "Ask Master, as he should know. So please ask him." Then, she brought the test to me during dinner.

So I took a look at it and thought, "All right. I can answer eighth-grade English problems as soon as I read them." But actually, I was puzzled even after spending some time reading through them, and I began to break out in a cold sweat. I thought to myself, "It's difficult. I don't know the answers. What goes in the blanks? This can't be happening." The only memory I had of eighth-grade English was that I got full marks on the tests, so there was no way I could not answer those questions. But considering her school was a prestigious one, I broke out in a cold sweat, thinking I had to relearn English grammar again.

So in the morning, I began to study a 400–500-page textbook on English grammar, which was probably a textbook that students used to study for university entrance exams. Back then, we had breakfast at 7:10 am. Because my children had to get ready for school, 7:10 am was when I had my breakfast. About 15 minutes before that, I went to the dining room and read the 400–500-page textbook and marked the important parts with red lines.

Because of all the experience I had with English, I could relearn it quite quickly. I went through the textbook three times in one year, including the practice problems, and after that, I could easily solve my daughter's English test when she brought it to me the following year. Further, I saw that her teacher overlooked a few problems in her grading. The teacher was a graduate of Waseda University, Department of English Language and Literature, and was in her first year of teaching. Upon seeing her miss a few problems, I thought she needed to study more. She went to NOVA (a popular school for introductory English conversation), so it was obvious she could not grade tests on English conversation.

Even at age 45, after studying English grammar for a year, I could spot the mistakes in the teacher's grading. That is how much I was able to improve my English skills. It is true that I had something to build on, and after I relearned what I had forgotten, I could solve the problems at a glance. That made me realize I could still do well if I studied.

Later, at 47, I fell ill and was hospitalized. After I was released, I needed to do some walking rehab, so I walked my daughter to her English conversation school and joined the class when I had free time. Then, she wrote, "I was astonished to know that even a 50-year-old person goes to an English conversation school." I was surprised that she would write such a thing. Who says a 50-year-old person cannot go to school to learn English conversation? I would never think that way.

At the trading company, even the people in their 50s and 60s used English. The company president, who was over 60, made speeches in English in front of an American audience. So he could not afford to make mistakes.

On one occasion, when the people in lower positions were writing a business plan, they wrote the company slogan as "X *For* Y"; in reply, the president ordered, "*For* is wrong. It's *To*. Change it to *To*." I wondered, "Is it *To* or *For*? I'm not sure. But we have no choice, as the president is telling us to change it to *To*." So we changed the business plan's slogan to "X *To* Y." Everyone was changing it from *For* to *To*, saying, "The 68-year-old president says it's *To*, so I guess it's *To*." I have forgotten the details, but the president used to live in the United States for over 20 years, so he must have been somewhat proficient in English. So just being older did not mean you could be incompetent at English. The older you were, the more others expected you to be proficient in English and the more often you needed to make speeches.

By the way, the content of your conversations about work will be quite advanced, so the knowledge you had as a young student will not help you at all in business negotiations.

Therefore, the older you are, the more you must know about various things.

## Precise and specialized English skills needed at the trading company

During my days at the trading company, I used to work in the Foreign Exchange for Exports (forex) section, where I read tens of thousands of English documents. Earlier, in Section 2 of this chapter, I talked about the task of photocopying at the Ministry of Finance; similarly, I read tens of thousands of pages of English documents and typed out documents in English. I used an English typewriter to type contracts and other documents in English, and I could not afford to make any mistakes. Numbers, dates, or whatever the document included—I could not make even a single mistake. Speed was demanded of me, but I could not make any mistakes; I had to be precise. That helped me to develop my work abilities.

Getting back to the main point, you must try to utilize the good aspects of what you have experienced and trained in and apply them to other areas. You should also make efforts to expand your capacity by building on your knowledge, experience, and advising ability. You need to grow slowly but steadily.

I am not sure how well I could do on exams, but seeing how I have produced over 100 books of the *Kuro-obi Eigo* series, if I were to look at a university entrance exam now, I would probably think it is easy. Or that is what I want to believe, at least.

Let me tell you about NHK's new radio program on business-level English conversation. A new lecturer is now teaching this course. NHK categorizes the English used in European and American societies into several levels: A, B, and C, with C1 being the top level in the radio program. And among the example sentences mentioned in the program, I tried to look for a few good ones, but to tell the truth, they were all at the level I used to read when I had just entered the trading company. Sentences of this level are ranked the most difficult, but they are all worthless. You won't be able to do any work if your English is only at this level. I thought to myself, "The business-level English sentences selected by a teacher of English conversation are at this level of difficulty. But there is a much tougher, much higher level of English. What they chose are sentences that a new employee will see when they have just started working." But I guess they were targeting a wide audience.

By the way, the forex section I was in received contract papers from the company's all 20 sales headquarters. We had to turn those contracts into trade documents and then into money, so we needed to be able to understand the contents of the contracts sent to us by the 20 sales headquarters. So whether the contract was about food, chemicals, lumber, machines, carts, ramen, missiles, or anything else, we could not overlook a single detail—it was specific information about the cargo that was hauled onto the ship. It was my job to check those things. Honestly, a graduate of the Faculty of English Literature probably would not understand any of the English written in those contracts. And I was checking those contracts. Then, the sales department or the delivery department prepared documents in English.

We handled imports as well as exports. Let us take exports as an example. First, the sales department signs a contract with the client. Then, the item purchased by the client is given to the shipping company for exporting, and the client sells it to collect the money. However, it takes a while for the client to receive the item and sell it for money, so we at the forex section turn the contract into a trade document, take it to the bank along with a promissory note, and have the bank pay us a discounted amount.

Suppose that we can collect our money 90 days after the client receives our goods. We issue a 90-day promissory note, along with a forex document, and take it to the foreign exchange section at the bank. And if the document is prepared without any errors, the bank will pay us the money for our goods with the 90-day interest discounted. So the money comes in even though our goods have yet to reach the client. And with this money, we can pay our sales department. That is what I used to do at the trading company.

# 7

# The Importance of Making Decisions

## Aim to become a topflight worker in your main work

There are various goods being imported and exported. Nowadays, we see robots being used, but even before they came along, we needed to be able to read documents on similar themes, so I took a wide interest in all kinds of imports and exports.

Some people might not trust me because they think I am "technologically incompetent," but let me tell you something. When CASIO built a factory in New Jersey, across the river from New York, I was one of the people who created the system to import its products into Japan. Many of you may have used CASIO calculators before. I was involved in establishing the import route. Although I could not drink beer, I could import beer bottles. Likewise, although I was not very good at using calculators, I could create an import route for calculators.

I was also involved with computers. I did not understand them very well, but I was involved in the importing and exporting of early-model computers. When banks began to implement computers as a part of their new online system, I was involved with that, too.

Therefore, I believe I am naturally quite adaptable. But we must never forget our main line of work. We must remember where our wages or income comes from. We absolutely need to be topflight in our main line of work.

Aside from our main line of work, we should learn about other topics because the more extra knowledge we have, the more it will help us. Why do we need to gain knowledge? It is to make decisions. We cannot make decisions regarding things we do not know. That is why we need to know. If we know about many things, we can make decisions. This is a very important point. Developing a higher level of decision-making ability is the best way to improve your ability to do practical work.

## Doing well at practical work will help you to gain the trust of others

I have written a few novels over this past summer (2021), and many of you may have read them. I have received some of your comments.

I have read books written by other novelists—in particular, the graduates of the University of Tokyo, such as Soseki Natsume, Ryunosuke Akutagawa, Yasunari Kawabata, and Yukio Mishima. I read their novels for learning and confirmation.

When Shio, my aide, read my novels, she told me, "Your novels are always logical, and they always have a clear conclusion. But when it comes to novelists, their stories often have no conclusion." I asked her whether my fantasy-like novels are similar to those of fantasy authors such as Kafka or Kenji Miyazawa, a poet and agricultural instructor who wrote *Night on the Galactic Railroad*. But she told me, "No, their stories have no logic or conclusion, whereas all of your novels do." I thought, "Oh, I see. I guess that is how people feel when they read my novels." She is right.

I do not write about things without a message or conclusion. I believe this is a quality that has been effective in my work and comes from my study of law at university and the practical work I did at the trading company. This tendency exists even in the fantasy-like stories I write.

Simply put, these things give Happy Science its trust. The trust I receive as a person, as well as the trust Happy Science receives as an organization, comes from the fact that we are trustworthy in terms of worldly work.

## The more spiritual you become, the more worldly effort you will need to make

In addition, extra added value comes from being able to make a judgment about how you perceive the information that is not of this world. It is tough to make a decision about whether you should believe in what a spirit is saying. You cannot easily tell where the spirit is from or who the spirit really is. It might be someone other than who it claims to be.

As we, Happy Science, conduct our activities, more people will develop spiritual abilities. What will be extremely important about them is whether they are living and working properly as human beings. If people who are not living and working properly hear the words of a spirit, they will only pick out the parts that are convenient for them and will stray from the right path. This is where mistakes will happen.

Thus, people who do not make mistakes doing ordinary tasks or people who can make correct decisions when doing practical work can also make the right judgment on what a spirit says. They can make a decision by thinking, "Does it make sense? Does it sound odd? Is it trying to mislead me? Is it trying to shift the topic of discussion without me knowing?"

In short, this is what I want to say. Those who have not studied and are incompetent in worldly work will not be able to work as proper psychics. I want to tell you, "You will probably make mistakes. At first, heavenly spirits may come down to you, but you won't be able to notice when you become possessed and manipulated by evil spirits. Many leaders of big religious groups have gone down this path.

Often, what those people have in common is that they did not study enough." People who are incompetent at work will do as the spirits say, and they often take the wrong actions. This is an important point.

Imagine those who arrive at the wrong conclusions, make the wrong, opposite decisions, or make decisions and take actions that others have to clean up after. When these people hear a spiritual voice or opinion, see spirits or visions, or experience other spiritual matters, they will most likely misinterpret them in a similar way as they misinterpret worldly matters. In particular, psychics deal with other-dimensional matters, and as decisions regarding these matters cannot be made based on the logic of this earthly world, it is very easy to make mistakes. In fact, the more spiritual you become, the more you must refine your abilities and not make wrong decisions regarding worldly matters.

Those who can understand what kind of person is speaking and how credible their opinions are in this world can also correctly understand what the spirit is saying. But those who cannot tell the speaker's level and credibility or those who mishear and pick up only what is convenient for them and arrive at the opposite conclusions will misinterpret what the spirit is saying. So what I want to say is that if these types of people become involved with religion, they will only mislead people.

## You need to have common sense and make an effort to do good work

The same goes for things involving extraterrestrial beings. Space people are currently contacting Happy Science. Many other people may also be saying things such as they have heard of, seen, or met space people. These people are rarely acknowledged by the public media, although some of them may.

Again, what is important is whether you, as a person, have the ability to make sound judgments. For example, are you able to tell whether a person is odd or decent by listening to him or her speak? Space people will presumably speak of things you have not heard of, but if you cannot judge whether a person is odd or decent, it will be very tough to tell whether what space people are saying is sound or not. Are you living properly with a pure heart? Are you making responsible decisions? This is an essential point.

Back in the day, "living recklessly" meant being hooked on alcohol, women, and mahjong. Nowadays, it means doing drugs and having all kinds of paraphilia, among other things. Either way, you must know that high spirits will never come down to those who just live recklessly in this world. That is why those undergoing spiritual discipline are told to live righteously and observe the precepts. Please be careful regarding these points.

There will probably be more people who can see spirits or hear their words. I would like to say to those people that you must first read and study our basic teachings as well as put effort into acquiring common sense. Let me make this clear: You must develop your abilities and put in the effort to keep doing good work—in other words, to extend your working years. People who are not prepared and trained in this way will have no excuse when they lose their jobs.

I do not know the details, but currently, there seem to be many companies in decline. If I were asked to go to one of those companies and work as a CEO every day, I wouldn't; but if I were consulted on what is wrong with the company, I could probably point out the problem. After observing all the work done at the company and talking to its employees, I could probably make a judgment as a management consultant.

As you can see, there is no end to how much a person can develop, so please continue to learn.

# 8

## How to Stay Active in Your Career

### Take to heart that you will forget the things you have learned

Also, even when you think you have learned something, you will forget it. You will definitely forget. It cannot be helped; you will forget. When you learn something new, you will forget the old knowledge. When you think you have forgotten a lot or you feel that you should re-study something, please study it again. This is important.

When I was in my 20s, I could still answer the university entrance exams by just glancing through them, but it became tough when I reached my 30s. Once you begin studying various things through work and learn more things, you will find that what you have learned through exam studies will be "sunk." There will be other knowledge from work piled up on it, so it will not be readily available; you will only have a faint memory of it.

Please forgive me if I sound like I am discriminating against certain people, but in the worst case, your intellect might even drop to the level of a student at a women's junior college that does not require an entrance exam and where students are knitting in the front row during class.

As you study other fields, your memory may fade; for example, you might forget the chronological order of the Kamakura, Heian, and Muromachi periods in Japanese history. This happens when you study other things. You will experience this in many other areas.

You may forget geography as well. You might think, "Umm, where was this?" "Which prefecture was it?" "Which country was it?" "Norway is in the southern hemisphere, right?" These are "danger" signs. So once you start thinking like this, you should go back and study those things again.

For instance, you could casually read through a couple of pocket-sized educational books such as Iwanami Shinsho paperbacks or Kodansha's new library of knowledge. Even by only doing that, you can recall some of your memory. If you want to study more, you should read proper books. But in any case, please do not forget the fact that humans will forget.

The same can be said of younger people; it can also happen in your 20s. Let us assume you passed Grade 1 of EIKEN (an English proficiency test). But that does not mean you will only improve from then on. If you take the exam again two years later, you may fail. Your ability really declines, so you will forget it all before you know it.

I have heard that you get a simple pass or fail nowadays in EIKEN. Back in my days, there were more rankings, such as Not Passed (A rank), Not Passed (B rank), and Not Passed

(C rank). I, too, retook the exam a couple of years after I passed it and found that my English skills had drastically deteriorated. I remember thinking, "What? I passed this a few years ago, but this time, I got 'Not Passed (C rank).' Oh, my goodness, most of what I have learned has 'vaporized.' I have to be stricter with myself." You really do forget within just a year or two, so please do not forget that humans have this tendency. If you want to extend your career, you should summarize what I have said above and take it to heart.

## Do not become "tengu the conceited" but become a bodhisattva

Another point I would like to make is that you should continue to take an interest in new things, regardless of your age. Please live with this thinking. Do not become full of yourself too soon. Those who think like this will fail quickly.

I understand how younger people feel. If you are outstanding in your teens or 20s, you want to be accepted right away. "Approve of me already and treat me in a way that others will know it as well"—I truly understand such a feeling, but if you are treated that way, you will fail after that. You will have no future. That is what you should fear. Therefore, before you become full of yourself, you need enough time to discipline and prepare yourself, and you should always reflect on the things you need to work on.

During my days as a student, I constantly reflected on myself, thinking, "I've become 'tengu the conceited.' I'm always boasting and looking down on people, thinking I'm better than everyone else." I reflected on myself a lot and thought of myself as an immature person. But when I read the novels I had written after 40-plus years, I did not think I was so conceited. I did not make up lies in my novel, so I was not tengu. I was not conceited at all, so I wondered why I was so caught up thinking and was reflecting on it a lot.

Regarding this, my aide, Shio, told me, "Master, when you thought you had said something that hurt someone, you reflected on it and regretted it. Younger people nowadays are not like that. They are complaining and grumbling about how they were hurt by what others said to them. They always talk about how they were hurt by others. On the other hand, you were very concerned about how you may have hurt others. This can be seen in your novels and also in other books. That is the difference." Well, as the saying goes, "Lookers-on see most of the game." I guess what she said is true, and it made sense to me. I kept reflecting on the things I thought I should not do but could not stop myself from doing them.

However, younger people nowadays often vent their anger, saying, "He didn't approve of me. She gave me a bad assessment. He spoke ill of me. She scolded me for doing poor work. This is a 'black' company (a company with exploitative working conditions)!" This is how they respond—the younger people from the *yutori* (pressure-free) generation, whose textbooks are half the size of what they used to be. But they must know that they are being easy on themselves.

Do not become tengu so easily. People who easily become conceited are self-centered and are only interested in themselves. They stress over how much they were hurt, and they are satisfied as long as they can boast about themselves. But if you do not understand other people's feelings, you will not become a bodhisattva. No matter how smart you may be, you will not become a bodhisattva, let alone a tathagata, if you do not understand other people's feelings. It means you will be below such high spirits. Being smart will only take you up to the sixth dimension at best. You must also know that your state of mind might be poor; there is a chance that you might end up in hell, or you might simply end up reincarnating within the Realms of Desire.

Also, some people in their 20s might think they can get through life by controlling or manipulating others or by putting on many different faces and deceiving others. I will say to those people, "That is an overly optimistic view of life. This is not a practice match in a dojo. If this were a 'real' match, you would be killed in one hit. That is how tough life is." Please be aware of this.

## Continue to work on your inner self to become a first-rate person

Let me give you an example. Some actors may think it is enough to remember the script once they receive it and manage to act as it says. I think these actors are second-rate or even third-rate. As for true actors, once they expect they will receive an offer for a character, they will establish the mentality needed for the role, do the necessary physical training, and get to a first-rate level. Those who can polish themselves like this every time they get a role are true actors.

If you think you can fool the audience by just acting the part, you may be successful for some time but not forever. You may think you are using all kinds of techniques, but you are actually just doing the same old thing every time. That is why you must continue to study.

It may be OK for you to just act in romantic movies or TV series when you are still young and beautiful, but once you reach the age of 30, you will have to play different roles—perhaps a judge, a prosecutor, a lawyer, a mayor, or a politician. Just because you read a script does not mean you can play the role of a politician or a prosecutor. You must take an interest in society, read newspapers, and read relevant books. You cannot grow further unless you prepare your brain for it.

So I suggest you stop yourself from easily becoming tengu. Escalators will not always take you upward; they can take you downward, too. There are escalators going in both directions. If you get onto a descending one, you will not ascend no matter how much you walk upward. You will just keep descending. Not many people realize this. In most cases, they lack the enthusiasm to study and, therefore, become conceited tengu. This applies to various genres.

Happy Science is now talking about matters such as extraterrestrial beings and UFOs, and about *The Laws Of Messiah* (2022), which is of a very high level. So, I was worried that Happy Science believers would forget our basic teachings and be misunderstood as odd by others. That is why I deliberately made this chapter so long.

I hope you can get a hold of what I wanted to convey. I would also like you to understand through the novels that I wrote in my younger days how I had been thinking at that time.

CHAPTER THREE

# Spiritual Ability and the Right Way of Life

## —The study of humans in the new era

Originally recorded in Japanese on March 2, 2022,
at the Special Lecture Hall of Happy Science in Japan
and later translated into English.

# 1

# The Difficulty of Discerning Good and Evil in Spiritual Matters

This chapter is a lecture I gave to celebrate the 31st anniversary of Happy Science officially becoming a religious corporation. The Tokyo Metropolitan Government approved us on March 7, 1991. From time to time, although not every year, I give a commemorative lecture for this occasion.

This chapter is titled "Spiritual Ability and the Right Way of Life." The general public working and living in society may not be very interested in this topic. But this will be an important theme for Happy Science staff or believers who are studying my teachings.

In particular, when I look at other religious groups, I notice that some people achieve the status of a teacher by simply developing spiritual ability. However, actually, it is a little more complicated than just labeling someone with spiritual ability a "teacher."

Back when Happy Science was trying to establish itself as a religion and was publishing spiritual messages, I spoke with the president of the publisher that handled our spiritual messages. He said, "As for new religions, a well-known psychic-based group has 1,200 psychics." But this figure is a little hard to believe; the group probably thinks that if a member experiences a spiritual phenomenon, he or she is a psychic. This group practiced esoteric Buddhism.

When I had just opened my spiritual channel, I also met someone who belonged to another religion. He told me, "If we wear a spiritual ornament called *omitama*, we can expel the evil spirits possessing us by casting our hand over each other." I will refrain from mentioning the group's name.

He told me, "We sit facing each other and read a sutra. Then, we cast our hand and remove the evil spirits possessing each other." So it seems that a person under possession is removing the other person's evil spirits and vice versa. They are doing this face-to-face in a dojo. Logically speaking, this does not sound right.

An established person with the power to expel spiritual beings can indeed remove an evil spirit possessing someone. But it is a little ignorant to think that those possessed by evil spirits can remove an evil spirit from another person. They may be swapping their evil spirits with each other, but this level of perception shows that their spiritual power is very low.

You may be able to feel something spiritual come down to you, but to determine whether the spirit is good or evil or the spirit's level or identity, you will have to go through advanced spiritual discipline. It is not easy. These are the difficult things regarding spiritual matters.

# 2

# Focusing More on Your Inner-Self Rather Than on Appearance

## Many people are actually interested in spiritual matters

I am living among the general public today. I dress in "disguise" and stroll outside in an outfit I do not want our believers to recognize. You will find me wearing a down coat, a hat similar to an ushanka, a scarf, a mask, and glasses. The outfit makes me look like an average middle-aged man, so I casually take a walk or go shopping. Sometimes people notice me, but most times, they do not.

The other day, I went to a cafe with my wife, and when we were having a cup of tea, the following happened. This cafe is usually very empty, but on that day, about six ladies from a luxury condominium nearby sat behind us and had some cake and tea. I heard them saying things like, "I can see ghosts," "I felt something touching me," "I got the chills," and "I called for an exorcism." They went on and on about such things, so I thought they perhaps recognized me, but then again, it seemed they were talking about someone else.

I do not know them, so I am not sure if they knew an exorcist or if one of them was an exorcist herself. But the cafe owner serving them tea said, "Oh, I'm sorry, I didn't know you were so famous." Perhaps one of those ladies was an exorcist. Indeed, quite a few ladies are interested in spiritual matters. They were enjoying their time chatting about how it is natural for spirits to exist in this world and cause spiritual disturbances and how people can see or feel the spirits or walk past them. I heard this and thought many people do have such spiritual experiences.

I, on the other hand, listened to them while trying not to talk about spiritual things myself. Sometimes we might have mentioned specific names, so we had to be careful about that.

As you can see, it is not easy to tell who in this world likes, knows, has an interest in, or is involved in spiritual matters.

## Happy Science has been focusing on its content since the beginning

It is easy to tell whether someone is involved in spiritual matters if they look the part. For example, by looking at what a monk is wearing, you can tell whether he is daisojo (a Buddhist priest of the highest order) or of another rank.

There was a religious group that once caused a huge problem in Japanese society. The group became a religious corporation about one and a half years before Happy Science—we were approved in 1991, and they were approved in 1989.

People showed an image of the leader of this religious group and me, side by side, on a television program, so I was quite troubled by that. In the program, people were asking why I was wearing a suit, but the leader of the infamous group walked around the city wearing a shabby, plain-colored robe similar to a sari that Buddhist monks wear. They were debating about why I was wearing a suit.

One of the commentators on the show, named Koichi Hori, the head of Boston Consulting Group at the time, said, "It's easy. Ryuho Okawa only has experience as a businessman, so he's just wearing what he used to wear. People who have been practicing religion prefer to wear religious clothes. That is the only difference." People seemed convinced and surprised by this. In this way, generally, people cannot differentiate between religious groups.

When Happy Science first started out, our headquarters and branches were based in rented-out rooms of buildings, which meant there were also other offices and shops there. If we went about the building dressed in odd clothing, other people would think negatively of us, so we did try to blend in. For example, we wanted to avoid making others feel uncomfortable when bumping into us on the elevator. That is why we kept ourselves in line with the general public.

Later on, when we started having lecturers, they wore a simple religious stole. Some even wore a holy item bound by a cord like a necklace, though I, myself, did not wear it. Our lecturers wear those holy items when they conduct a ritual or give a lecture; otherwise, they do not wear them at most times. In this way, when Happy Science first started, we tried not to stand out but blend in with the public owing to worldly circumstances.

We started off by establishing our publishing department, and people working in bookstores were relieved to see us visit in a suit. But regarding the aforementioned religious group that committed murder, they said, "The people in that group come and walk around the bookstore dressed like an Indian ascetic. We felt so uncomfortable and troubled." That is another reason our staff is dressed in suits. It comes from my own experience.

That being said, you can easily deceive and be deceived by others based on appearance. However, you should know that appearing to be enlightened does not mean you are enlightened. For this reason, Happy Science has been competing based on its content from the very beginning.

Early on, when we held our special lectures at Tokyo Dome, my holy robes were made just for the occasion. It took us a very long time to make one. People would start working on the robe months before, and it was always completed right before the event. A robe, crown, scepter, and other things were made, but they always arrived at the last minute, so they could not be altered.

For example, when I told the staff that the crown was heavy when I wore it, they glued the crown to my head so it would not fall. But that in itself became another big challenge. I previously had the chance to try on the bride's wig at a Japanese-style wedding. It weighed about two kilograms (four to five pounds) and was very heavy, so it was not easy to bow with the wig on; the crown felt the same. I was bothered by its weight, and it prevented me a little from concentrating my mind so that spirits could come down into me.

Now, the El Cantare statue is made to look like it is wearing a holy robe, but in reality, I place more importance on practicality. I believe that I can concentrate more on the content of the work by keeping the outfit simple.

## Why I dismissed the idea of a uniform

In the early days of Happy Science, the staff only wore formal wear—a formal black suit for both men and women, which was convenient, as you could also wear it for weddings and funerals. But I have to say it felt a little odd. When they came to see me, they all wore black. When they held a meeting at Tokyo Shoshinkan (a seminar facility for Happy Science) for branch managers, they all came wearing black. It looked like they were either attending a funeral or a wedding, but everyone was in black, so I remember saying, "Something feels off."

Also, I have had many requests for a uniform. A female staff who used to work for JAL (Japan Airlines) asked me to make a uniform for all staff. It would look smart if everyone wore a uniform and dressed the same, but that is possible because those jobs hire people who can fit into its image. Such jobs choose those who look smart and orderly in a uniform so that others would admire them. That is why they look stylish despite wearing the same clothes.

But that was not the case for us. So I said, "Everyone has a unique character, so perhaps they should wear what matches their character." Thus, I did not say yes to the idea of a uniform. And that may be why the Laws of Beauty, which is one of the three criteria of Buddha's Truth—Truth, Goodness, and Beauty—survived.

# 3

## Fighting Off Spiritual Hindrance and Ensuring Quality Control

### I seemed like a bookworm but had a surprising skill in my student days

Thinking back, I probably had a good sense of colors and shapes. It must have come from my family line. There were relatively many artists and sculptors in my family line, so I also had such artistic ability. There is no point in saying this now, but in my junior high school years, for some reason, I was the best at art, such as drawing pictures, and technology and home economics, such as technical drawing and crafts.

My grandfather was a master builder of shrines, although I am not sure if that is a genetic trait. Also, my father sometimes took up drawing, and I, too, could draw and craft quite well and made accurate technical drawings. As for technical drawing, it must come from my family line. I could draw a perfect one; I was able to accurately gauge depth and shapes. I am not sure whether this is genetic, so you will have to ask a geneticist about it. But to my surprise, I had a skill in such a field. At the moment, I still have not used much of this skill, and it may or may not surface before I die. Anyway,

I had an unexpected hobby, preference, and interest in those fields.

I am truly humbled that nowadays, I publish poems, *tanka* and *haiku* (both short poems), and compose music. To tell the truth, I have not received any special training in related fields. Many of our staff members used to be in a band and spent much of their younger days playing music. They wanted to become a professional musician but could not, and they became our staff instead. I was not that type of person but was rather a bookworm who spent much of my time reading books. That is how people perceived me, and it may be true.

But I do think I have some kind of musical sense as well. For instance, I used to get a full score in fill-in-the-blank questions of musical notes. I do not know why. It has been a long time since I last read sheet music, so I cannot read the notes now, but back then, I could easily fill in the blanks. I had such an ability. So once I heard the piece, I could write out all the melodies. But after all the studying I did for entrance exams and other circumstances, this ability remained unused and dormant.

## Some will spiritually awaken
## by studying my books and lectures

I am now publishing the amateur novels I wrote when I was younger. But some of our staff members commented, "Master, you probably would have made it as a novelist or a writer." What lovely disciples, I thought; I have to pat them on their heads. But in reality, I did not have much confidence.

I remember my aunt (Shizuko Nakagawa), who was a writer, made ¥3,000 per page. It must have been tough to keep writing manuscripts for such a deal. If IRH Press were to pay me ¥3,000 per page now, I would be quite rich. I cannot calculate how much I would make, as I do not know how many pages I wrote. But considering all the books I published, if I were to vertically stack all the manuscripts, they would probably be higher than Mt. Fuji. I think I wrote enough scripts to surpass it.

Everyone has talent in different things; people who gather to religions also have various kinds of talent. Some may have high academic achievements, and some may not. All kinds of people gather to religions, each person taking a different route.

As these people listen to my lectures, conduct rituals, or take seminars, some will spiritually awaken and develop spiritual intuition. For example, they might be able to tell, at a glance, whether an evil spirit or an *ikiryo* (evil spirit of a living person) has possessed someone. They might also feel something heavy on their shoulders and think that a spirit has come to them. Or they might think, "The man I met today must have had something possessing him." When these people with spiritual intuition visit certain "power spots," they might think to themselves, "My body feels heavy whenever I come here," or "I feel the light comes shining into me when I come here." Sometimes it is hard to tell whether a power spot is good or bad, but when you develop spiritual intuition, you will be able to feel such "power."

Looking back at the extensive work I have done to this date, I have published over 2,950 books, including translated titles, and I have given over 3,400 lectures, with over 1,250 officially recorded spiritual messages (at the time of this lecture; this book is the 3,000th book. As of April 2023, more than 3,100 books have been published and more than 3,500 lectures have been recorded, with over 1,300 officially recorded spiritual messages and readings). I do not keep count of unofficial sessions, so there may be over 10,000 if I include those. In any case, I have been accumulating my achievements.

In addition, the lectures I gave when I was younger can still be listened to, published, and studied. The content has not gone out of date for the current youth who enter Happy

Science to learn. It may seem like I am randomly getting my hands on everything, but I have been steadily building up on my achievements. That is how I work.

## The feeling of a "spiritual current" running through you

Some people are aware of their own spiritual abilities as psychics. Others may not realize their abilities but develop spiritual abilities as they learn at Happy Science for a long time. Sometimes people develop spiritual abilities shortly after they join the group. Among those people, some can consciously use their abilities, whereas others cannot. But in any case, it is very difficult for people studying at Happy Science to remain uninfluenced by and insensitive to spiritual matters.

If they are spiritually insensitive, it is as if their souls are encased in very thick ice. Unless the ice surrounding them melts away, spiritual light will not reach the core of their soul. This may be the case for completely inactive members or someone who only joined because their family or relatives are Happy Science members. Nevertheless, as they read my books and listen to my lectures, the encasing or the outer layer will start to melt, and the core of their souls will appear.

Let me explain more clearly. When you reach the state where you feel a spiritual current run through you, it means you can grasp the existence called the mind within you. You will be able to tell what kind of state your mind is in. You will be able to see the state of your mind as if you are looking into a crystal ball.

You will be able to objectively observe the state of your mind. For example, you will be able to think, "I'm feeling agitated now," "I'm so angry and restless," or "I feel calm now." Or you can tell, "Now I'm wishing this person well," "I'm acting cunningly to gain something," "I'm trying to draw this person toward my side," or "I'm being calculative."

Therefore, it is rare for you to be completely free of spiritual experiences. At the least, you will dream when you are sleeping. While you are dreaming, you will probably experience something that is not of this world. As you get involved with religion, you will more closely interact with the Spirit World.

The simplest form of that occurs when you are sleeping at night. During your sleep, your soul often detaches from your physical body and travels to the other world. While this occurs, your soul and physical body are still connected by a thin cord known as the Silver Cord that extends from the back of your head. Even then, you may not go to a special place in the Spirit World if you are just living an earthly way of life. You will most likely go to a place where other spirits of living people are wandering.

But if you have gone through a horrifying or painful experience in this world, it will not be so difficult for you to experience hell (in the other world). For example, you may sometimes have a terrifying dream, a colorful dream, or a dream where you can touch things or another person as if they are real. In those cases, you have probably traveled to the Spirit World.

However, you will not be able to go up to the truly higher world, the higher realms of the heavenly world—namely, the world of gods. This is a matter of course. You must complete sufficient spiritual discipline to be able to go there. A wall separates the higher dimensions from the lower dimensions of the Spirit World, and you usually cannot get past the wall no matter how hard you may try.

Therefore, although you can leave your body when you are dreaming, you will most likely be wandering within the Realm of Desires. In other words, you are among the spirits who still have worldly desires and are repeatedly reborn into this world based on such desires.

## An open spiritual channel does not mean almighty power

I have given more than 3,400 lectures since I started doing this work, and the most difficult challenge in delivering them is maintaining my spiritual condition. This is extremely difficult to do.

It would be easier if I did not have to interact with others at all, but that is not possible. While living in this world, I have to interact with at least a few people. I see them every day, talk to them, and engage with them at work. I also meet people on the street when I go outside, visit a department store, visit shops, or dine at restaurants. You will meet various people. So if your spiritual ability is solely passive, oftentimes, you are easily influenced by the people you encounter.

When I was a university student, I did not think that my spiritual channel was open. But when I got home from busy places such as Shibuya or Shinjuku, many times, I felt as if my body got heavier. Crowded areas tend to have many evil spirits, and I probably came in contact with them and took them home with me.

I believe that is why I preferred to take a walk in the park. Anyway, even when evil spirits followed me home, as I deeply and meditatively read books that spiritually cultured me in my apartment, they gradually left. Also, whenever I proactively made time to read books I could tune into, which meant they were written by angels of light and great guiding spirits of light, my mind eventually attuned to their wavelength. Then, the troublesome spirits I met in cities had no choice but to leave, as they could no longer be on the same wavelength as me.

What was the toughest in this world was working at a company office. Working there came with restrictions, such as not being able to choose who I stood next to on the commuter train or sat next to at the office because we had assigned desks. These scenes have also been portrayed in the Happy Science movie, *Twiceborn* (executive producer and original story by Ryuho Okawa, 2020). In reality, I felt very uncomfortable working near someone who was spiritually disturbed. I remember thinking back then, "This world is a tough place. It's very taxing."

On the contrary, once I resigned from the company and decided to start a religion, I could quickly detach myself from such negative spiritual influence. Even so, ever since establishing Happy Science, I had been giving personal counseling sessions, and sometimes I gave a teaching on people's common worries and problems that were seen in those counseling sessions. Therefore, I was susceptible to people's pain and suffering.

When we first started Happy Science, even the executive staff who closely worked with me lacked spiritual training. They happily worked as long as I praised their work, but as soon as I scolded them for their mistakes and admonished them for making wrong decisions, they immediately felt offended and angry. In most cases, they then became spiritually disturbed. For example, someone who had been fine until the previous day became possessed after I scolded them. It is quite tough to work with someone who is under a negative spiritual influence. It truly is.

It was especially tough when the person I saw right before my lecture was spiritually disturbed. Such people really do interrupt my concentration, so dealing with that was difficult. After giving a few thousand lectures, I can say that quality control, which involves delivering lectures without being spiritually interrupted, is the most difficult task.

It is also particularly difficult to live peacefully without causing any friction among the circle of people you cannot avoid making contact with. You must make efforts to live like that. That is why it is completely wrong to assume you are almighty once you open your spiritual channel and can hear the voice of spirits.

# 4

## Spiritual Ability Must Come with Greater Insight and Learning

### A psychologist cannot medically examine someone more highly regarded than them

In most cases, psychics communicate with their own guardian spirits only, but those spirits are not almighty. Yet some psychics think they can be spiritual teachers as long as they can converse with these spirits. But if truth be told, guardian spirits can only recognize as much as the psychics would if they themselves were to return to the other world. I discovered this point early on. Communicating with your guardian spirit is not enough; you must attain a higher state of spirituality.

As you may have seen in our movies, when I started channeling spiritual messages while I still worked for a company, I considered the high spirits as greater beings than I was and listened to them. But after I renounced the secular life and focused on spiritual discipline to attain enlightenment, I myself became a professional, so the positions between the high spirits and myself began to reverse. You can see how difficult it was to portray this in our movie. When I first began communicating with high spirits, some spirits of the bodhisattva level spoke to me with authority, like a teacher. But as my level of spiritual awareness rose, our positions reversed. These things are not easily experienced.

The teachings of the bodhisattva level are good enough to save the general public. In fact, their teachings are probably easier for people to understand than the teachings of the tathagata level and beyond, which are grand laws that cover greater issues affecting the entire human race, ethnicity, or nation. Therefore, tathagatas and above will have to speak on such topics. This is the difficult part.

That is why you need to acquire greater insight. This is very important. Everyone must have a certain level of insight regardless of their spiritual abilities. How much you can understand others depends on the level of your insight. If you have a higher level of insight than those around you, you can easily see through and point out their thought processes and actions. But there are many people who are more highly regarded than you in this world. In that case, it is difficult for you to understand what they are thinking or trying to do.

This also applies to psychologists when they give advice. Usually, in psychiatry and such, doctors examine patients with mental disorders. They also write various books, but they mainly see patients with mental illness. They advise the patients and work hard to identify their problems and restore them to their healthy state.

On the contrary, some of their patients are more respected than they are in this world, so they cannot give advice to those patients. This matter has long been troubling psychiatrists, and it seems that Alfred Adler felt something had to be done about it. If you are dealing with patients all the time, you would feel like you are a god. But there are many people who are more respectable than you in this world, and in such cases, you can neither understand their feelings nor give them advice. That means you must go through more discipline and raise your own level of insight.

Let us take hens, for example. Hens full of energy grow large because they are smarter in how they eat than other hens. The question is whether you can spot the difference between those hens. Similarly, for you to be able to explain why someone succeeded, you must know about all kinds of things and know many different types of people. You must not deal with just patients; you must also learn about various societies that other people live in.

## Answering questions on topics
## from management to black holes

Until you open your spiritual channel, you must make efforts to form an extremely pure, transparent, and crystallized mind.

Unless you brush away impurities and dirt from your mind and make it transparent, the light of God or Buddha will not come down to you. But once you become a professional spiritual leader, you must keep studying various things. You will not be able to give answers about things you do not know.

Recently, I have been publishing a series of Q&A sessions that we always held at lecture events during the early years of Happy Science. Even as I read through them now, I think some questions are quite difficult. Many of them are probably difficult for our lecturers to answer.

I used to hold an hour-long Q&A session at the venue after giving an hour-long lecture. Eventually, I held Q&A sessions in front of 10,000 people, and I had no idea what kind of people were in the audience. It would have been better if people had asked me questions related to the lecture. The MC did ask the audience to base the question on the lecture every time, but even then, people kept asking irrelevant questions and consulted their personal worries. The questions got very irrelevant, which made me think, "What? What does this have to do with the lecture I just gave?" But in any case, I did my best to answer them as I thought each question was important to those people.

For example, I would answer a question from a CEO on how to rebuild a company and then answer a question about the black hole. Such a thing happened many times. I was once asked, "I've heard that only large celestial bodies turn into black holes and that the sun is not big enough to form a black hole; it must be larger to form a black hole. Is this really true?" I guess this person worked in the field of science. I responded right away, "No, it's not true. Something the size of Earth can become a black hole if it shrinks down to 1.77 cm in diameter." This is not something that can be answered with just spiritual inspiration. I had been studying the latest physics in my everyday life, so I could answer such a question when it came out of the blue.

As for the question about rebuilding a company, you would need to have studied management in general. But you also need to consider what would happen if COVID were to spread widely or if a war were to start. When you are in such unusual times, you must think about how to modify the management know-how that you were taught.

## The required studies to offer opinions to various leaders

Sometimes I will need to do things that go beyond my job scope. Mr. Kuroda, the governor of the Bank of Japan, has been serving in the position for several years now (at the time of this lecture). But before he became the governor, the position remained vacant for some time. I myself harshly criticized the previous governor—I saw that he was doing the opposite of what should be done and voiced that what he was doing was wrong.

The previous governor had studied supply-side economics, or economics focused on increasing the money supply to control the economy. But he went along with the nature or culture of the Bank of Japan, which has been to fight inflation. So he regulated the supply of cash and currency and raised interest rates to prevent inflation. Seeing this, I thought, "Now is not the time to prevent inflation. The economy is not growing at all; don't you know that? You were studying for your Ph.D. in economics at the University of Chicago (he had received his MA), but you don't understand this?"

I felt I sounded rude when criticizing someone of a "Ph.D. level in economics," as I am a graduate of the faculty of law. Nevertheless, the reality was that the interest rates had to be dropped and the currency supply had to be increased. As a man who had actually been working in the international economy, I clearly criticized him. Then, he was later dismissed. Speaking of the Bank of Japan, when my current wife started working there as a new employee, it had no governor. It was an unusual situation.

In this way, I must give opinions to such an extent sometimes. Or I must offer my opinion to the prime minister of Japan or even the president of another country. I feel reluctant to speak out to them because I am not in a position to do that; nevertheless, I state what is on my mind. At the very least, you need as much knowledge as a top-tier journalist or critic to speak on matters that involve a country's leader. If you speak out without having enough knowledge, you are getting out of line. That is why you must study to get to a high level.

While I was using my spiritual abilities for religious activities, I was also teaching people how to undergo spiritual discipline and about the spiritual world. Although those were the main activities, I was also studying various other fields. I spent a very long time simultaneously studying numerous topics. I kept studying related subjects until I had enough knowledge to give my opinion on them. This was a challenge. So the Q&A sessions we conducted in our early years were a stimulating experience for me. You should think about the kind of questions people might ask in this day and age, and that is why you must study different genres and be prepared to answer various questions.

# 5

# A Religious Professional Must Be a Person of Great Culture and Knowledge

## Stating your thoughts while keeping in mind the opposite opinion

In terms of how I think, I am not the type of person who only reads what is in line with my way of thinking. Although I have my own thoughts, I read and analyze a wide range of opinions, from exactly the opposite to very similar ideas. I try to maintain a balance and give my opinion while being aware of the opposite opinion in my mind.

This is the difference between myself and my disciples— the lecturers. My disciples tend to only take my conclusion and force that onto people, which is why people oppose them. In my case, I state how I arrived at such a conclusion. I would say, "Based on this reasoning, there are options A, B, and C, but after considering them all, I believe option A is the best choice. That is what I think." There is a premise and a process before I arrive at my conclusion.

However, my disciples only take my conclusion; they simply echo what I say like a parrot, and many people are not convinced by it.

In the early days of Happy Science, a Christian member joined us—he is now one of our directors. Back then, his father, also a Christian, read one of my disciple's opinions that deemed Christianity an evil religion. Then, the father got angry and said, "Master Okawa does not say Christianity is an evil religion."

I have accepted Christianity and acknowledged the work Jesus did, but I also say, "Christianity isn't good enough as a modern religion because it lacks certain teachings, so Christians should change their way of thinking." I point out what is lacking in Christian teachings, such as how they do not teach about past lives, do not recognize the difference between God and high spirits, and do not understand the concept of soul siblings. I teach about the thinking that Christians should have. But my disciples only take what I pointed out as being deficient in Christianity and label it as a misguided religion.

On a similar note, Soka Gakkai used to publish something called *Shakubuku Kyoten* (a guide for preaching down). It was a compilation of mistakes made by various religions, and Soka Gakkai members could go out doing missionary work with just this single book. What they did was they went up to someone from another religious group and pointed out the mistake of that group. For example, if a member meets someone who believes in Japanese Shinto, he would say, "You are mistaken because Japanese Shinto started the Pacific War."

Merely memorizing what to say would make you similar to those members of Soka Gakkai, but in that case, you would also create many enemies.

## What was lacking in the leaders of new Japanese religions?

In that sense, a religious professional must be a person of great culture and knowledge, but there is also no end to accumulating such qualities.

In Japan, many founders of new religions were uncultured—for example, an uncultured, middle-aged female farmer was struck with an illness but heard the voice of God after she recovered from it. Another founder heard the voice of God when misfortune fell on their family member. You can find many such cases in new religions. Also, many of these founders were only as educated as high school dropouts. Many of them were like that; thus, in a way, the founders who did not study so much accepted or listened to the voice of God more easily. Among them, those who were not misguided probably had pure hearts. Thus, the less they studied, the easier it was for them to receive spiritual revelations. If they had too much knowledge, it would prevent them from hearing the voice of God.

Around the time when Happy Science was founded, scholars that studied new religions spoke of Seicho-no-Ie and GLA as "religions of intellects." I am sure the founders did study, but in the worldly sense, I could not agree.

Mr. Masaharu Taniguchi, the founder of Seicho-no-Ie, dropped out of the English Studies preparatory program at Waseda University. Nowadays, it would probably correspond to dropping out in the first year of university. He could read easy English, but his translations were not very accurate; his translated work was of poor quality. He used to write, "There was someone named Edgar Kai-shee." He called Edgar Cayce "Edgar Kai-shee." Also, I could not understand some of his translations.

In addition, Seicho-no-Ie teaches, "All religions emanate from one universal God." But if we look at the content of its teachings, we can understand the phrase to mean, "All religions converge into Seicho-no-Ie."

However, even though the group advocated this idea, Taniguchi mistakenly wrote in 1930: "Shakyamuni was the prince of Magadha...." And even around 1985, he still did not correct it. This proved that he did not study. Shakyamuni was not the prince of Magadha; Ajatasatru was the prince of Magadha. Shakyamuni Buddha was the prince of a small kingdom called Shakya, which was a vassal state of Kosala. What Taniguchi had written in 1930, before World War II, was not corrected even in 1985 or so. It may still be uncorrected even now. Thus, that was as much as he studied.

Another example is Shinji Takahashi, the founder of GLA. Apparently, he was outstanding as an engineer. He ran a company that produced bearings used for breaks in shinkansen (bullet trains). But whether he graduated from the College of Science and Technology at Nihon University is questionable. His profile is written as if he graduated from there, but perhaps he did not. It also suggests that he studied at the University of Tokyo after graduating from the College of Science and Technology at Nihon University. However, this is also quite hard to believe, as it is a very unusual course.

Takahashi often said, "Even if you don't study, you will know." He meant to tell everyone not to study because if they did, they would discover he had little knowledge. That is why he said, "I won't study. I opened my spiritual channel, and I can hear the voice of my guardian spirit, so that makes me a spiritual teacher." However, although he wrote of himself to be Buddha's rebirth, I felt he had only read about two rows of bookshelves worth of books on Buddhism. I could tell so after I read his books and spotted his inconsistencies.

He also talked about Christianity, but it seemed he had only read *The Life of Jesus* by Tadao Yanaihara. I believe it is difficult to develop rightful recognition unless you study up to a certain point.

## Intelligence alone does not make you a good religious leader

Then, would having a high deviation score, or a high educational background, and being praised by others for being smart and intelligent in the worldly sense make you a good religious leader? Not necessarily. Much of the knowledge you learn in school is junk in terms of the Truth, and it can prevent you from learning the Truth.

For instance, you may learn in school that a dead frog twitches when you apply electric shock to its legs or thigh. Then, the teacher might explain, "This is due to muscle contraction, not because it is alive." A similar explanation can be provided to humans. People in a vegetable state or a brain-dead state sometimes move their hands or legs or shed tears when they hear their families talking about them. Nevertheless, doctors who practice medicine based on materialism would say, "Their nerves and muscles are showing a reflex response. It sometimes happens. But they are not alive. It doesn't mean they've come back to life."

At the least, the level of medical science is far from the Truth in the Spirit World. Psychology partially involves spiritual science, but people in psychology are trying their best to make it a non-religious matter. In most cases, they just use medicine to deal with psychological problems. In fact, they have no idea what is really going on.

Carl Jung was a psychic, and when Jungian psychology first came into being, it was described as a "new religion conducting activities in the mountains." It is now becoming a field of study, but it cannot completely prove the existence of the Spirit World. In truth, Jung himself had many spiritual experiences, but his psychology did not reach this level of spirituality. Therefore, I believe many people have been incorrectly diagnosed.

# 6

# Be Humble and Take One Firm Step at a Time

## Do not become tengu for having spiritual abilities

So you must keep studying. Unless you have a clean, transparent mind, you will not be able to receive spiritual revelations, so you have to maintain such a mind. In addition, you must keep studying and try to maintain a healthy physical body. A poor physical condition can make you susceptible to negative spiritual influence. These cumulative efforts will lead you to live a sound life.

Even if you have spiritual abilities, people will focus on how you go about your daily life to see if you are living the right way. If a psychic always says peculiar things and acts in a strange manner, they will be deemed odd by those around them. Psychics may possess spiritual abilities, but if they are living a reckless life or hanging out with troublemakers, you can tell they are attracting bad spirits. No heavenly spirit will come down to them. Therefore, it is important to be humble and take one firm step at a time.

Also, as you continue to deepen your study on a specific topic, you may feel like you have become an expert on it.

But if you become tengu (a conceited person), that would be the end. Being conceited makes you drop your guard. When you become tengu, you will desire fame. When this desire is born, you will value people who flatter you but will be enraged when others point out your mistakes or criticize you. You will not be able to see others correctly.

That is why there are two different types of smart people. Even egoists can get good grades, get into a good school, or get into a good company. In fact, the more egoistic you are, the more likely you will get better scores. Being an egoist will also work in your favor to get a job; some would even use their connections and information to get the desired job.

The same goes for cram schools and prep schools. They tell you, "We will teach you this part only. It will definitely be on your next exam!" And you would feel smarter when you get good grades. But in reality, you did not achieve these grades through your own effort. Therefore, although it is better for you to be outstanding, you must also be humble and make even more efforts to advance further.

People who have grown conceited will no longer listen to other people's opinions. There is plenty of knowledge to learn outside of school studies in this world, and many people have much more experience than you, so you should lend an ear and learn from what they have to say. But those who are proud of themselves think that doing well in school means they have learned everything. This is unfortunate. Having too much pride will halt you from making further progress, so you should avoid becoming tengu.

## The consequences of using your intelligence for selfish reasons

Some clever people use their intelligence to deceive people, lie, cover up the truth, or frame others. You might have read about such people in stories of Japanese feudal eras or military strategies. And yes, they do seem smart. But if these cunning people use their intelligence for the wrong reasons, angels will not want to guide them.

Please excuse me for citing a fragmentary episode, but let me give you an example from the Japanese television drama series, *The 13 Lords of the Shogun*. Masaki Suda played the role of Yoshitsune. In the drama, there is a scene where Yoshitsune shoots an arrow and kills a rabbit. But another person also shoots an arrow and insists that his arrow was the one that killed the rabbit. So they start fighting over who got the rabbit. Then, Mr. Suda (playing Yoshitsune) says, "OK, let's shoot an arrow as far as we can. The one who can shoot further is the winner, and he will take the rabbit." The other man shoots an arrow quite far, but he sees Mr. Suda standing still with an arrow in his hand. He asks, "What are you waiting for? Aren't you going to shoot your arrow?" Mr. Suda then says, "Sure," and he turns toward the man and shoots him with the arrow, killing him. And he took the rabbit home.

The drama probably wanted to portray Yoshitsune as a good military strategist. I understand that it was fiction. But if everyone used their brains for that kind of purpose, this world would be a tough place to live in. It would be like a world described in *Julius Caesar*, in which Caesar said, "Et tu, Brute?" You would never know when someone close to you or who served near you will backstab you.

If you frequently use your intelligence for the wrong reasons, then you will probably not receive guidance from bodhisattvas, angels, or tathagatas. You might be guided by spirits from hell—or if not them, then by tengu, *yokai*, *youma* (bewitching spirits), or sorcerers at best. In some cases, you might even be influenced by satans of hell.

Therefore, you will eventually be disliked by others and will stop yourself from making further progress if you use your cleverness for selfish desires only—in other words, using your intelligence to benefit yourself only. Of course, you should not deceive people, frame them, or give them false information to get what you want. These are not something angels and bodhisattvas should do.

You may do well on worldly exams, but that does not mean you have high spiritual grades. People may graduate from the same university, but they are all different in nature. Some may be like angels, whereas others are the opposite— like devils. Please be careful on this point.

## Religion is a comprehensive study of humans

Therefore, it is important to discipline yourself and live each day with humility, knowing that God and Buddha are always watching over you.

I understand it is natural for you to harbor a strong desire to protect yourself, but you must check to see if you are protecting yourself out of self-love, like how animals and insects behave. Are you protecting yourself for the sake of manifesting God's Will on earth, or do you just want to be praised or boast about yourself? It is important to always be aware of these things.

I often use the example of water in a bathtub. It is a simple example, but very, very few people understand what it means. When you push the water in the tub away from you, the water comes back toward you. But when you pull the water toward you, the water will move away from you. This is an example used by Sontoku Ninomiya. It is very simple, but very few people understand it, indeed. You might try to draw water toward you, hoping to get more water for yourself. However, the more you draw it, the more it flows away from you in the opposite direction.

Although it is a simple analogy, people think, "But I would lose out if I give to others. I would gain by taking more. It's wiser to think that way." That may be true in terms of competing to survive. Squirrels, for example, stuff as many walnuts as they can in their cheek pouch and store them in their nest to survive. Smart squirrels know where to bite on the walnut to crack it. If you study zoology, you will find that foolish squirrels spend a lot of time cracking walnuts because they do not know where to bite; but wise squirrels know where to bite so that they can quickly and efficiently crack walnuts and eat them. There seems to be such a difference between these squirrels.

In terms of your own survival, it is important to keep more for yourself. However, such thinking is not sufficient for many people to live together and improve their lives. Of course, you must establish yourself first, but that is not the end; the path continues. As the next step, please know that it is important to be useful to others and cooperate with others.

No matter how smart you may be, if you have zero cooperative skills, you cannot work at a company. An exception might be if you have the ability, like Edison, to invent new things and contribute to society through your inventions. Otherwise, you cannot work at a company if you are unwilling to cooperate with others. Not a single person can become the president of a company right away. The reason you fail to become president is that you cannot endure the years before reaching the top.

Therefore, it is important for you to think that religion is a comprehensive study of humans and make an effort. Moreover, please keep studying the knowledge you need to use directly in your work; at the same time, slowly but steadily accumulate other indirect knowledge that you might not immediately use. In addition, please constantly make efforts to discern your main subject of study from others— discerning the trunk of a tree from the branches of the tree. These are essential things.

Out of concern, I spoke about "Spiritual Ability and the Right Way of Life." I believe some of you are already aware of your spiritual abilities, whereas others are not aware even though they have such power. Either way, please recall what I talked about from time to time and remind yourself not to be conceited but humbly continue to make efforts.

# *Afterword*

I am still not thinking of the number of books I aim to publish during my lifetime.

I just only wish to continue enlightening the people of the world.

Happy Science has now spread to over 165 (168 as of April 2023) countries. I am happy that my books are being read in each country and in each language. However, whether my teachings have universality that envelops the world depends on my day-to-day effort.

May as many people as possible awaken to the Truth and live with faith in God.

Whatever unhappiness may fall upon humanity, may they see the light of hope that the Savior is living in the same age as them now.

May the sins of humanity be forgiven and the earth be filled with love.

May many angels and bodhisattvas be nurtured in this current age, too.

I am publishing this book for the world, wishing for the happiness of the people of the whole world.

May there be lots of happiness!

*Ryuho Okawa*
*Master & CEO of Happy Science Group*
*April 29, 2022*

*For a deeper understanding of*
The Road to Cultivate Yourself
*see other books below by Ryuho Okawa:*

*The Laws of the Sun* [New York: IRH Press, 2018]

*The Laws Of Messiah* [New York: IRH Press, 2022]

*Shakyamuni Buddha's Future Prediction* [Tokyo: HS Press, 2020]

# ABOUT THE AUTHOR

Founder and CEO of Happy Science Group.

Ryuho Okawa was born on July 7th 1956, in Tokushima, Japan. After graduating from the University of Tokyo with a law degree, he joined a Tokyo-based trading house. While working at its New York headquarters, he studied international finance at the Graduate Center of the City University of New York. In 1981, he attained Great Enlightenment and became aware that he is El Cantare with a mission to bring salvation to all humankind.

In 1986, he established Happy Science. It now has members in 168 countries across the world, with more than 700 branches and temples as well as 10,000 missionary houses around the world.

He has given over 3,500 lectures (of which more than 150 are in English) and published over 3,100 books (of which more than 600 are Spiritual Interview Series), and many are translated into 41 languages. Along with *The Laws of the Sun* and *The Laws of Hell*, many of the books have become best sellers or million sellers. To date, Happy Science has produced 27 movies. The original story and original concept were given by the Executive Producer Ryuho Okawa. He has also composed music and written lyrics of over 450 pieces.

Moreover, he is the Founder of Happy Science University and Happy Science Academy (Junior and Senior High School), Founder and President of the Happiness Realization Party, Founder and Honorary Headmaster of Happy Science Institute of Government and Management, Founder of IRH Press Co., Ltd., and the Chairperson of NEW STAR PRODUCTION Co., Ltd. and ARI Production Co., Ltd.

# WHAT IS EL CANTARE?

El Cantare means "the Light of the Earth," and is the Supreme God of the Earth who has been guiding humankind since the beginning of Genesis. He is whom Jesus called Father and Muhammad called Allah, and is *Ame-no-Mioya-Gami*, Japanese Father God. Different parts of El Cantare's core consciousness have descended to Earth in the past, once as Alpha and another as Elohim. His branch spirits, such as Shakyamuni Buddha and Hermes, have descended to Earth many times and helped to flourish many civilizations. To unite various religions and to integrate various fields of study in order to build a new civilization on Earth, a part of the core consciousness has descended to Earth as Master Ryuho Okawa.

**Alpha** is a part of the core consciousness of El Cantare who descended to Earth around 330 million years ago. Alpha preached Earth's Truths to harmonize and unify Earth-born humans and space people who came from other planets.

**Elohim** is a part of the core consciousness of El Cantare who descended to Earth around 150 million years ago. He gave wisdom, mainly on the differences of light and darkness, good and evil.

**Ame-no-Mioya-Gami (Japanese Father God)** is the Creator God and the Father God who appears in the ancient literature, *Hotsuma Tsutae*. It is believed that He descended on the foothills of Mt. Fuji about 30,000 years ago and built the Fuji dynasty, which is the root of the Japanese civilization. With justice as the central pillar, Ame-no-Mioya-Gami's teachings spread to ancient civilizations of other countries in the world.

**Shakyamuni Buddha** was born as a prince into the Shakya Clan in India around 2,600 years ago. When he was 29 years old, he renounced the world and sought enlightenment. He later attained Great Enlightenment and founded Buddhism.

**Hermes** is one of the 12 Olympian gods in Greek mythology, but the spiritual Truth is that he taught the teachings of love and progress around 4,300 years ago that became the origin of the current Western civilization. He is a hero that truly existed.

**Ophealis** was born in Greece around 6,500 years ago and was the leader who took an expedition to as far as Egypt. He is the God of miracles, prosperity, and arts, and is known as Osiris in the Egyptian mythology.

**Rient Arl Croud** was born as a king of the ancient Incan Empire around 7,000 years ago and taught about the mysteries of the mind. In the heavenly world, he is responsible for the interactions that take place between various planets.

**Thoth** was an almighty leader who built the golden age of the Atlantic civilization around 12,000 years ago. In the Egyptian mythology, he is known as god Thoth.

**Ra Mu** was a leader who built the golden age of the civilization of Mu around 17,000 years ago. As a religious leader and a politician, he ruled by uniting religion and politics.

# BOOKS BY RYUHO OKAWA

## Recommended Titles

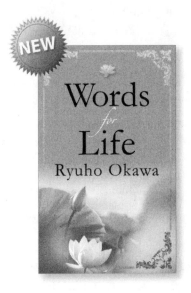

## Words for Life

Paperback • 136 pages • $15.95
ISBN: 979-8-88727-089-7 (Mar. 16, 2023)

"I hope you'd take some time to flip through this book on the train, bus, or before you go to sleep, and meditate on the phrases and reflect on yourself."                    -From Afterword and Commentary

Ryuho Okawa has written over 3,100 books on various topics. To help readers find the teachings that are beneficial for them out of the extensive teachings, the author has written 100 phrases and put them together in this book. Inside you will find words of wisdom that will help you improve your mindset, change you into a more capable and insightful person, and lead you to live a meaningful and happy life.

## What Is Happy Science?

Best Selection of
Ryuho Okawa's Early Lectures Vol.1

Paperback • 256 pages • 17.95
ISBN: 978-1942125-99-0

These are the historical records of Ryuho Okawa's series of passionate public lectures which he gave in front of more than 2,000 people during the ages of 32 and 33, each time on a different subject including enlightenment, self-realization, and the multi-dimensional universe and without a single script, the second to third year after establishing Happy Science.

## The Challenge of Enlightenment

Now, Here, the New Dharma Wheel Turns

Paperback • 380 pages • $17.95
ISBN: 978-1-942125-92-1 (Dec. 20, 2022)

Buddha's teachings, a reflection of his eternal wisdom, are like a bamboo pole used to change the course of your boat in the rapid stream of the great river called life. By reading this book, your mind becomes clearer, learns to savor inner peace, and it will empower you to make profound life improvements.

## Latest Laws Series

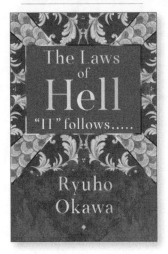

## The Laws of Hell

"IT" follows .....

Paperback • 264 pages • $17.95
ISBN: 978-1-958655-04-7 (May 1, 2023)

Whether you believe it or not, the Spirit World and hell do exist. Currently, the Earth's population has exceeded 8 billion, and unfortunately, 1 in 2 people are falling to hell.

This book is a must-read at a time like this since more and more people are unknowingly heading to hell; the truth is, new areas of hell are being created, such as 'internet hell' and 'hell on earth.' Also, due to the widespread materialism, there is a sharp rise in the earthbound spirits wandering around earth because they have no clue about the Spirit World.

To stop hell from spreading and to save the souls of all human beings, the Spiritual Master, Ryuho Okawa has compiled vital teachings in this book. This publication marks his 3,100th book and is the one and only comprehensive Truth about the modern hell.

# El Cantare Trilogy

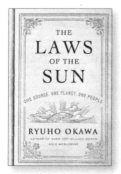

### The Laws of the Sun

One Source, One Planet, One People

Paperback • 288 pages • $15.95
ISBN: 978-1-942125-43-3 (Apr. 20, 2021)

Imagine if you could ask God why he created this world and what spiritual laws he used to shape us—and everything around us. In *The Laws of the Sun*, Ryuho Okawa outlines these laws of the universe and provides a road map for living one's life with greater purpose and meaning.

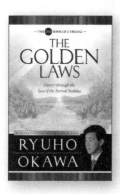

### The Golden Laws

History through the Eyes of the Eternal Buddha

E-book • 204 pages • $13.99
ISBN: 978-1-941779-82-8 (Sep. 24, 2015)

Throughout history, Great Guiding Spirits of Light have been present on Earth in both the East and the West at crucial points in human history to further our spiritual development. *The Golden Laws* reveals how Divine Plan has been unfolding on Earth, and outlines 5,000 years of the secret history of humankind.

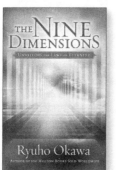

### The Nine Dimensions

Unveiling the Laws of Eternity

Paperback • 168 pages • $15.95
ISBN: 978-0-982698-56-3 (Feb. 16, 2012)

This book is a window into the mind of our loving God. When the religions and cultures of the world discover the truth of their common spiritual origin, they will be inspired to accept their differences, come together under faith in God, and build an era of harmony and peaceful progress on Earth.

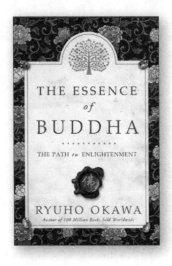

## The Essence of Buddha

The Path to Enlightenment

Paperback • 208 pages • $14.95
ISBN: 978-1-942125-06-8 (Oct.1, 2016)

In this book, Ryuho Okawa imparts in simple and accessible language his wisdom about the essence of Shakyamuni Buddha's philosophy of life and enlightenment–teachings that have been inspiring people all over the world for over 2,500 years. By offering a new perspective on core Buddhist thoughts that have long been cloaked in mystique, Okawa brings these teachings to life for modern people. *The Essence of Buddha* distills a way of life that anyone can practice to achieve a life of self-growth, compassionate living, and true happiness.

## The True Eightfold Path

Guideposts for Self-Innovation

Paperback • 256 pages • $16.95
ISBN: 978-1-942125-80-8 (Mar. 30, 2021)

This book explains how we can apply the Eightfold Path, one of the main pillars of Shakyamuni Buddha's teachings, as everyday guideposts in the modern-age to achieve self-innovation to live better and make positive changes in these uncertain times.

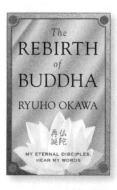

## The Rebirth of Buddha

My Eternal Disciples, Hear My Words

Paperback • 280 pages • $17.95
ISBN: 978-1-942125-95-2 (Jul. 15, 2022)

These are the messages of Buddha who has returned to this modern age as promised to His eternal beloved disciples. They are in simple words and poetic style, yet contain profound messages. Once you start reading these passages, your soul will be replenished as the plant absorbs the water, and you will remember why you chose this era to be born into with Buddha. Listen to the voices of your Eternal Master and awaken to your calling.

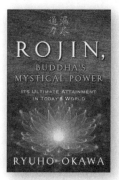

## Rojin, Buddha's Mystical Power

Its Ultimate Attainment in Today's World

Paperback • 224 pages • $16.95
ISBN: 978-1-942125-82-2 (Sep. 24, 2021)

In this book, Ryuho Okawa has redefined the traditional Buddhist term *Rojin* and explained that in modern society it means the following: the ability for individuals with great spiritual powers to live in the world as people with common sense while using their abilities to the optimal level. This book will unravel the mystery of the mind and lead you to the path to enlightenment.

## The New Genre of Spiritual Mystery Novel
## - The Unknown Stigma Trilogy -

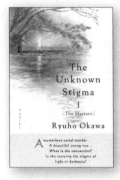

### The Unknown Stigma 1 <The Mystery>

Hardcover • 192 pages • $17.95
ISBN: 978-1-942125-28-0 (Oct. 1, 2022)

The first spiritual mystery novel by Ryuho Okawa. It happened one early summer afternoon, in a densely wooded park in Tokyo: following a loud scream of a young woman, the alleged victim was found lying with his eyes rolled back and foaming at the mouth. But there was no sign of forced trauma, nor even a drop of blood. Then, similar murder cases continued one after another without any clues. Later, this mysterious serial murder case leads back to a young Catholic nun...

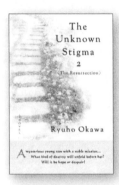

### The Unknown Stigma 2 <The Resurrection>

Hardcover • 180 pages • $17.95
ISBN: 978-1-942125-31-0 (Nov. 1, 2022)

A sequel to *The Unknown Stigma 1 <The Mystery>* by Ryuho Okawa. After an extraordinary spiritual experience, a young, mysterious Catholic nun is now endowed with a new, noble mission. What kind of destiny will she face? Will it be hope or despair that awaits her? The story develops into a turn of events that no one could ever have anticipated. Are you ready to embrace its shocking ending?

### The Unknown Stigma 3 <The Universe>

Hardcover • 184 pages • $17.95
ISBN: 978-1-958655-00-9 (Dec. 1, 2022)

In this astonishing sequel to the first two installments of *The Unknown Stigma*, the protagonist journeys through the universe and encounters a mystical world unknown to humankind. Discover what awaits her beyond this mysterious world.

## Other Recommended Titles

The Ten Principles from El Cantare Volume I
Ryuho Okawa's First Lectures on His Basic Teachings

The Ten Principles from El Cantare Volume II
Ryuho Okawa's First Lectures on His Wish to Save the World

Twiceborn
My Early Thoughts that Revealed My True Mission

Developmental Stages of Love - The Original Theory
Philosophy of Love in My Youth

The Laws of Happiness
Love, Wisdom, Self-Reflection and Progress

The Laws of Secret
Awaken to This New World and Change Your Life

The Challenge of the Mind
An Essential Guide to Buddha's Teachings:
Zen, Karma and Enlightenment

The Power of Basics
Introduction to Modern Zen Life
of Calm, Spirituality and Success

Spiritual World 101
A guide to a spiritually happy life

*For a complete list of books, visit okawabooks.com*

# "The True Words Spoken By Buddha"

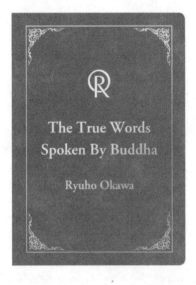

This is one of the greatest gospels for humankind; this sutra, which is the English version of Happy Science's basic sutra, was written directly in English by Master Ryuho Okawa.

Available to Happy Science members. You may receive it at your nearest Happy Science location. See pp.198-199.

# MUSIC BY RYUHO OKAWA

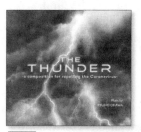

193

# ABOUT HAPPY SCIENCE

Happy Science is a global movement that empowers individuals to find purpose and spiritual happiness and to share that happiness with their families, societies, and the world. With more than 12 million members around the world, Happy Science aims to increase awareness of spiritual truths and expand our capacity for love, compassion, and joy so that together we can create the kind of world we all wish to live in.

Activities at Happy Science are based on the Principles of Happiness (Love, Wisdom, Self-Reflection, and Progress). These principles embrace worldwide philosophies and beliefs, transcending boundaries of culture and religions.

**Love** teaches us to give ourselves freely without expecting anything in return; it encompasses giving, nurturing, and forgiving.

**Wisdom** leads us to the insights of spiritual truths, and opens us to the true meaning of life and the Will of God (the universe, the highest power, Buddha).

**Self-Reflection** brings a mindful, nonjudgmental lens to our thoughts and actions to help us find our truest selves—the essence of our souls—and deepen our connection to the highest power. It helps us attain a clean and peaceful mind and leads us to the right life path.

**Progress** emphasizes the positive, dynamic aspects of our spiritual growth—actions we can take to manifest and spread happiness around the world. It's a path that not only expands our soul growth, but also furthers the collective potential of the world we live in.

## PROGRAMS AND EVENTS

The doors of Happy Science are open to all. We offer a variety of programs and events, including self-exploration and self-growth programs, spiritual seminars, meditation and contemplation sessions, study groups, and book events.

Our programs are designed to:
* Deepen your understanding of your purpose and meaning in life
* Improve your relationships and increase your capacity to love unconditionally
* Attain peace of mind, decrease anxiety and stress, and feel positive
* Gain deeper insights and a broader perspective on the world
* Learn how to overcome life's challenges
  ... and much more.

*For more information, visit <u>happy-science.org</u>.*

# HAPPY SCIENCE UNIVERSITY

## THE FOUNDING SPIRIT AND THE GOAL OF EDUCATION

Based on the founding philosophy of the university, "Exploration of happiness and the creation of a new civilization," education, research and studies will be provided to help students acquire deep understanding grounded in religious belief and advanced expertise with the objectives of producing "great talents of virtue" who can contribute in a broad-ranging way to serving Japan and the international society.

## FACULTIES

### Faculty of human happiness

Students in this faculty will pursue liberal arts from various perspectives with a multidisciplinary approach, explore and envision an ideal state of human beings and society.

### Faculty of successful management

This faculty aims to realize successful management that helps organizations to create value and wealth for society and to contribute to the happiness and the development of management and employees as well as society as a whole.

### Faculty of future creation

Students in this faculty study subjects such as political science, journalism, performing arts and artistic expression, and explore and present new political and cultural models based on truth, goodness and beauty.

### Faculty of future industry

This faculty aims to nurture engineers who can resolve various issues facing modern civilization from a technological standpoint and contribute to the creation of new industries of the future.

# CONTACT INFORMATION

Happy Science is a worldwide organization with branches and temples around the globe. For a comprehensive list, visit the worldwide directory at happy-science.org. The following are some of the many Happy Science locations:

## UNITED STATES AND CANADA

### New York
79 Franklin St., New York, NY 10013, USA
Phone: 1-212-343-7972
Fax: 1-212-343-7973
Email: ny@happy-science.org
Website: happyscience-usa.org

### New Jersey
66 Hudson St., #2R, Hoboken, NJ 07030, USA
Phone: 1-201-313-0127
Email: nj@happy-science.org
Website: happyscience-usa.org

### Chicago
2300 Barrington Rd., Suite #400,
Hoffman Estates, IL 60169, USA
Phone: 1-630-937-3077
Email: chicago@happy-science.org
Website: happyscience-usa.org

### Florida
5208 8th St., Zephyrhills, FL 33542, USA
Phone: 1-813-715-0000
Fax: 1-813-715-0010
Email: florida@happy-science.org
Website: happyscience-usa.org

### Atlanta
1874 Piedmont Ave., NE Suite 360-C
Atlanta, GA 30324, USA
Phone: 1-404-892-7770
Email: atlanta@happy-science.org
Website: happyscience-usa.org

### San Francisco
525 Clinton St.
Redwood City, CA 94062, USA
Phone & Fax: 1-650-363-2777
Email: sf@happy-science.org
Website: happyscience-usa.org

### Los Angeles
1590 E. Del Mar Blvd., Pasadena, CA 91106,
USA
Phone: 1-626-395-7775
Fax: 1-626-395-7776
Email: la@happy-science.org
Website: happyscience-usa.org

### Orange County
16541 Gothard St. Suite 104
Huntington Beach, CA 92647
Phone: 1-714-659-1501
Email: oc@happy-science.org
Website: happyscience-usa.org

### San Diego
7841 Balboa Ave. Suite #202
San Diego, CA 92111, USA
Phone: 1-626-395-7775
Fax: 1-626-395-7776
E-mail: sandiego@happy-science.org
Website: happyscience-usa.org

### Hawaii
Phone: 1-808-591-9772
Fax: 1-808-591-9776
Email: hi@happy-science.org
Website: happyscience-usa.org

### Kauai
3343 Kanakolu Street, Suite 5
Lihue, HI 96766, USA
Phone: 1-808-822-7007
Fax: 1-808-822-6007
Email: kauai-hi@happy-science.org
Website: happyscience-usa.org

## Toronto

845 The Queensway
Etobicoke, ON M8Z 1N6, Canada
Phone: 1-416-901-3747
Email: toronto@happy-science.org
Website: happy-science.ca

## Vancouver

#201-2607 East 49th Avenue,
Vancouver, BC, V5S 1J9, Canada
Phone: 1-604-437-7735
Fax: 1-604-437-7764
Email: vancouver@happy-science.org
Website: happy-science.ca

## INTERNATIONAL

## Tokyo

1-6-7 Togoshi, Shinagawa,
Tokyo, 142-0041, Japan
Phone: 81-3-6384-5770
Fax: 81-3-6384-5776
Email: tokyo@happy-science.org
Website: happy-science.org

## London

3 Margaret St.
London, W1W 8RE United Kingdom
Phone: 44-20-7323-9255
Fax: 44-20-7323-9344
Email: eu@happy-science.org
Website: www.happyscience-uk.org

## Sydney

516 Pacific Highway, Lane Cove North,
2066 NSW, Australia
Phone: 61-2-9411-2877
Fax: 61-2-9411-2822
Email: sydney@happy-science.org

## Sao Paulo

Rua. Domingos de Morais 1154,
Vila Mariana, Sao Paulo SP
CEP 04010-100, Brazil
Phone: 55-11-5088-3800
Email: sp@happy-science.org
Website: happyscience.com.br

## Jundiai

Rua Congo, 447, Jd. Bonfiglioli
Jundiai-CEP, 13207-340, Brazil
Phone: 55-11-4587-5952
Email: jundiai@happy-science.org

## Seoul

74, Sadang-ro 27-gil,
Dongjak-gu, Seoul, Korea
Phone: 82-2-3478-8777
Fax: 82-2-3478-9777
Email: korea@happy-science.org

## Taipei

No. 89, Lane 155, Dunhua N. Road,
Songshan District, Taipei City 105, Taiwan
Phone: 886-2-2719-9377
Fax: 886-2-2719-5570
Email: taiwan@happy-science.org

## Taichung

No. 146, Minzu Rd., Central Dist.,
Taichung City 400001, Taiwan (R.O.C.)
Phone: 886-4-22233777
Email: taichung@happy-science.org

## Kuala Lumpur

No 22A, Block 2, Jalil Link Jalan Jalil Jaya
2, Bukit Jalil 57000,
Kuala Lumpur, Malaysia
Phone: 60-3-8998-7877
Fax: 60-3-8998-7977
Email: malaysia@happy-science.org
Website: happyscience.org.my

## Kathmandu

Kathmandu Metropolitan City,
Ward No. 15, Ring Road, Kimdol,
Sitapaila Kathmandu, Nepal
Phone: 977-1-537-2931
Email: nepal@happy-science.org

## Kampala

Plot 877 Rubaga Road, Kampala
P.O. Box 34130 Kampala, UGANDA
Email: uganda@happy-science.org

# ABOUT IRH PRESS USA

IRH Press USA Inc. was founded in 2013 as an affiliated firm of IRH Press Co., Ltd. Based in New York, the press publishes books in various categories including spirituality, religion, and self-improvement and publishes books by Ryuho Okawa, the author of over 100 million books sold worldwide. For more information, visit okawabooks.com.

*Follow us on:*

f Facebook: Okawa Books     ⓘ Instagram: OkawaBooks

▶ Youtube: Okawa Books     🐦 Twitter: Okawa Books

𝓟 Pinterest: Okawa Books     g Goodreads: Ryuho Okawa

―――― **NEWSLETTER** ――――

To receive book related news, promotions and events, please subscribe to our newsletter below.

🔗 irhpress.com/pages/subscribe

―――― **AUDIO / VISUAL MEDIA** ――――

**YOUTUBE**        **PODCAST**

Introduction of Ryuho Okawa's titles; topics ranging from self-help, current affairs, spirituality, religion, and the universe.